Eleanor Roosevelt's World

The Library of

Crosby Hall

Tivoli-on-the-Hudson, where Eleanor Roosevelt spent her girlhood following the death of her parents. The mansion belonged to her maternal grandmother.

Eleanor Roosevelt's World

BY ROBIN McKOWN

PUBLISHERS Grosset & Dunlap NEW YORK

The permanent home of the United Nations on the East River in New York City — a monument to the ideal of world peace.

TO

Alice Thorne

Mrs. Roosevelt addresses the United Nations General Assembly on the tenth anniversary of the Declaration of Human Rights, December 10, 1958.

Foreword

The lifetime of Eleanor Roosevelt — from 1884 to 1962 — encompassed the horrible devastation of two world wars and any number of lesser ones, cropping up like forest fires first in one part of the globe, then in another. Dictators rose to power and fell, some fleeing to exile, others assassinated or killed by their own hands. New countries, proud and confident and hopeful of the future, emerged from centuries of bondage.

In this period the horse-drawn carriage gave way to the automobile. Travelers began to fly, by airplanes and the speedier jets. Atomic-powered submarines were launched, and finally man began to reach out toward the stars.

Electricity was tamed and, like an obedient genie, granted common citizens the miracle of electric light. Silent motion pictures were replaced by talking ones, in color. Radio and then television brought world events and mass entertainment even into the homes of the poor, while color TV made an entry as a luxury item.

The League of Nations, offspring of the First World War, perished ineffectively against the rising tide of fascism. The United Nations was born as a dream of President Roosevelt. It crystallized to a solid body, and in spite of setbacks and some failures became so staunchly a part of modern life that people forgot what it had been like before countries had a forum where they could air their grievances.

Women won the right to vote and entered hitherto forbidden fields where their intelligence and abilities fitted them. Their fashions changed radically, largely in the direction of comfort, all the way from the Gibson Girl silhouette of the 1890's to the blue jeans and sneakers of the supermarket shopper of the 1960's.

Most significant, in view of Eleanor Roosevelt's special interests, were the social changes during the seventy-eight years of her life. The wretched sweatshops in the New York of her childhood were abolished, little by little. Working conditions, for men and women, improved as labor grew stronger and more united. Old age pensions, unemployment insurance, and other social security measures, after a long struggle, were accepted as normal benefits which a government owes its working citizenry.

At last the hunger of the underprivileged was recognized as not merely a national problem but a world responsibility.

Eleanor Roosevelt, the child, wept at injustice. As she grew older, she spoke out against it, uncompromisingly and regardless of consequences. She opposed racial prejudice, child labor, discrimination against women, all forms of oppression. She strove for world peace and a greater tolerance among mankind. She was instrumental in formulating the Universal Declaration of Human Rights, one of the most important social documents in history. She gave her time, energy, money, wisdom, and the warmth of her compassion to needy individuals and worthy causes. When that was not enough, she persuaded others to give too.

In her many crusades she often encountered bitter opposition. No woman was ever more maligned, yet no one ever showed less resentment of slander. Multitudes adored her.

She continued fighting injustice, wherever she found it, until her death.

Contents

ACKNOWLEDGMENT

The author would like to give special thanks to Miss Elizabeth B. Drewry and Mrs. Joyce Millman, of the Franklin D. Roosevelt Library; Miss Josephine Motylewshi, of the National Archives; Miss Virginia Daiker, of the Library of Congress; Roy E. Johnson, of the American National Red Cross; Sidney Glazier, of the Eleanor Roosevelt Cancer Foundation; Lt. Col. Howard G. Stevenson, of the U. S. Army; Erwin van Swol, of the United States Information Agency; and to the staff of the Eleanor Roosevelt Foundation, for their generous cooperation.

Quotations on pages 23, 31, 39, and 47 are from *You Learn by Living* by Eleanor Roosevelt. Quotations on pages 71 and 79 are from *Autobiography* by Eleanor Roosevelt. By permission of Harper & Brothers. The quotation on page 55 is from *Long Shadow of Little Rock* by Daisy Bates, in the preface by Eleanor Roosevelt. By permission of David McKay Company.

For their courtesy and cooperation in supplying the pictures on the pages indicated, the author gives grateful acknowledgment to the following:

FRANKLIN D. ROOSEVELT LIBRARY: Front endsheet, pages 14, 16 (2), 17, 18, 20, 21, 22, 23, 26, 27, 32, 35, 37, 40, 41, 42, 48, 49, 50-51, 52, 57 (photograph by Cecil Beaton), 58, 68, 70, 72, 75, 76, 78, 83, 84.

WIDE WORLD PHOTOS: Pages 19, 31, 45, 46, 48, 56, 65, 66, 73, 74, 77 (2), 79, 82, 84, 85, 86, 89.

CULVER PICTURES, INC.: Pages 6, 15, 17, 19, 28, 30, 33, 36 (2), 43 (2), 53, 55, 61, 63, 64, 66, 87, 92.

UNITED NATIONS: Pages 9, 62, 90-91, 93, back endsheet.

CHARLES PHELPS CUSHING: Pages 24, 80-81 (photo by UN from Cushing).

PRESS ASSOCIATION, INC.: Page 67.

BROWN BROTHERS: Pages 26, 38, 39.

WHO PHOTO: Page 71

NATIONAL ARCHIVES: Pages 29 (Ad. Dept. General Staff), 59 (Navy Department), 60 (Defense Dept. Marine Corps), 67.

U. S. ARMY: Page 54.

COLLECTIONS OF THE LIBRARY OF CONGRESS: Pages 47, 56, 65.

Eleanor
Roosevelt's
World

I. Growing Up in the Victorian Age

"A human life is like a candle.
It is lit when a baby is born."

Her father was tall and bronzed, with sandy hair and a thick mustache. He had hunted tigers in India and, with his brother Theodore, had lived in the Wild West of the Dakotas. To his daughter, Elliott Roosevelt was a hero, the most perfect person in the world. Sometimes she danced for him, whirling round and round until he caught her in his arms, throwing her high in the air. "Little Nell," he called her, after the heroine of Dickens' *Old Curiosity Shop,* though her real name was Anna Eleanor Roosevelt. She was born in New York City on October 11, 1884.

"A funny child, so old-fashioned," her beautiful society mother, Anna Hall Roosevelt, said. In her presence Eleanor was tense and unsmiling, wishing that she dared touch her beautiful gown or jewels. "Come here, granny," her mother called to her once when they had company. Eleanor thought she would sink through the floor with shame.

She was two when her parents took her to see their distant relatives, the James Roosevelts, who lived near Hyde Park in a splendid mansion overlooking the Hudson River. Eleanor was left with four-year-old Franklin, who crawled around on all fours while she rode joyously on his back. She retained no memory of this first meeting with her future husband, but was told of it afterwards.

That year, October 28, 1886, the great Statue of Liberty was unveiled at Bedloe's Island in New York Harbor. "Give me your tired, your poor, your huddled masses yearning to breathe free," wrote Emma Lazarus of this tall, gracious lady holding a torch in her upraised hand.

Statue of Liberty.

For Eleanor's father, this golden-haired, blue-eyed child was "a miracle from Heaven."

Anna Hall Roosevelt, Eleanor's mother, was one of the most beautiful women in New York society.

Her handsome and charming father was brother to Theodore Roosevelt and godfather to another future American President — Franklin Delano Roosevelt.

In the decade of the 1880's some five million immigrants came to America's shores. Not all found the better world that the Statue of Liberty symbolized. Foreign women workers were employed in the garment industry for as little as three dollars a week. Children of the poor worked in factories, mills, and mines.

Once Elliott Roosevelt brought his tiny daughter to a Thanksgiving dinner given by rich society people for the newsboys of New York. He told her that these ragged gamins slept in empty lots or hallways. Her eyes filled with tears.

The next summer her parents took her and her small brother Elliott on their first trip to Europe. They rode in a gondola in Venice and tossed pennies into the volcano of Vesuvius. At Sorrento, she rode a little donkey along roads lined with olive and orange trees — that is, until she noticed that the donkey boy's bare feet were bleed-

ing. Then Eleanor made him ride and she walked.

Her second brother, Hall, was born in France. Their mother brought all three children back to America. Eleanor's father did not come nor did he ever again live with them. He had gone to stay in Abingdon, Virginia, and she saw him only at rare intervals.

"One day," he said to her on one of these occasions, "we will travel to far distant places. You and I together." With all her heart she believed him.

In 1889, when Eleanor was five, a young woman reporter, Nellie Bly, made a trip around the world for the *New York World* in seventy-two days, six hours, and eleven minutes. Many censured her for such unwomanly conduct.

Victoria, a righteous and capable woman, had been Queen of England since 1837. In both England and America, the Victorian Age would become synonymous for prudish morals and prim

[16]

manners. Wyoming was the only state in the Union where women had the right to vote. Susan B. Anthony, Elizabeth Cady Stanton, and a few other crusaders were campaigning for national woman suffrage under a barrage of ridicule from men and even some women. The English heroine of the Crimean War, Florence Nightingale, was an old lady of sixty-nine. Her example had inspired a number of daring young women to study nursing, among them Edith Cavell.

If a woman of good family had to work, she usually became a governess or a schoolteacher. Like most professions, writing was not considered a proper occupation for women. Emily Dickinson died in 1886, leaving unpublished the thousands of exquisite poems composed in her secluded life. The Brontë sisters and George Eliot had written their novels under male pseudonyms.

Women of achievement were not discussed in Eleanor's home. Beautiful women were the fortunate ones, she was taught. If one were plain, like herself, one had to strive doubly hard to cultivate good manners and make one's self agreeable to others.

She was eight when her mother died of diphtheria. With her brothers, she was taken to stay with her Grandmother Hall, who lived in a brownstone house on West 37th Street in New York City, and spent summers in her country place, at Tivoli-on-the-Hudson. Within a few months, Elliott, Eleanor's oldest brother, succumbed to scarlet fever. Two years later Eleanor was told that her father had died in Virginia. The triple loss in this brief period was too cruel to accept. For a long time she refused to believe in her father's death.

Grandmother Hall was convinced she had spoiled her own children. Eleanor's Aunt Pussie and Aunt Maude, for instance, actually rode in a hansom cab without a maid in attendance! To

"I am always questioning and questioning," teenage Eleanor wrote in her diary. "I can feel it in me sometimes that I can do much more than I am doing and I mean to try till I do succeed."

"I was not a happy child so I learned, earlier than most, how important the happy moments are."

*At the English boarding school of Allenswood, her schoolmistress, Mlle. Souvestre,
took a personal interest in her, taught her to think for herself. Eleanor is shown here
(middle row, second from left, seated) with her English classmates.*

make up for her indulgence, the old lady was extra strict with her grandchildren. Since she always said "no" instead of "yes" to their requests, Eleanor learned to ask for nothing to avoid disappointment. Cold morning baths were obligatory all the year round. She had to wear flannel underwear and petticoats and long black stockings from November through April, regardless of the weather. She had one girl friend who was allowed to visit her once each summer.

Formal education for girls was considered a waste, but from governesses she learned a smattering of grammar and arithmetic and became quite fluent in French and German. She read the novels of Sir Walter Scott and Dickens and other classics. Her preference was for sad stories. She was allowed to study ballet and was sent to dancing school, where she mastered the polka and the waltz.

Once in a long while her grandmother let her visit the Theodore Roosevelts at Sagamore Hill in Oyster Bay. She was always Uncle Teddy's favorite niece. "Bully to see you, Eleanor," he would say in his rasping voice, embracing her so wildly he tore buttons from her coat. Then he would lead her and his own brood in a series of madcap games all over the estate. But Uncle Teddy could be cruel too, without meaning it. To teach the children to swim, he insisted they jump off the dock into water over their heads. For Eleanor the ordeal was so terrifying it was years before she ventured into the water again.

At fourteen, she was invited to a party given by her Aunt Corinne for young people of her own age. The other girls wore fashionable floor-length gowns. Though she was taller than any of them, her dress reached just to her knees. Painfully wretched and self-conscious, she stood on the sidelines watching the couples glide by and trying desperately not to weep. Then a miracle happened. Her handsome young cousin, Franklin Roosevelt, whom she knew barely by sight, came over to ask for a dance. Never had she felt so grateful to anyone.

The next year she was sent abroad to the finishing school of Allenswood, outside of London, run by a Frenchwoman, Mademoiselle Souvestre. All conversation was in French, and Eleanor was able to help the English students who were less proficient in that language than she. For the first time she knew the heady pleasure of being esteemed and liked by other girls.

Mlle. Souvestre, with rare intuition, detected unusual qualities of mind and spirit in this awkward, badly dressed young American and took her under her wing. Eleanor was one of the chosen few with whom the headmistress discussed world affairs. From her, Eleanor learned of the Boer War in Africa between the English and the Dutch settlers, who were known as Boers, a group with whom Mlle. Souvestre privately sympathized. She also

Theodore Roosevelt – Eleanor's "Uncle Teddy."

Grandmother Hall did not wholly approve of the boisterous Theodore Roosevelts, but occasionally she permitted Eleanor to visit them at Sagamore Hill on Oyster Bay, Long Island.

told the girls of Captain Alfred Dreyfus, a French general staff officer of Jewish birth, who had been unjustly condemned as a traitor and who had spent five terrible years on Devil's Island before public indignation forced a retrial. The injustice of a big nation toward a small one; the injustice of society to an individual — these were lessons that Eleanor learned well.

At Mlle. Souvestre's instigation, Eleanor discarded the unbecoming clothes her grandmother had selected and used part of her modest allowance for stylish frocks. At Eastertime in 1901, the headmistress took her on a tour of the Continent. Eleanor became responsible for buying tickets and looking after the many trunks without which no lady of quality traveled. In Florence and Paris, Mlle. Souvestre encouraged her to visit museums and other historic places by herself, but word of these unorthodox excursions reached her grandmother, and she was ordered home.

The Spanish-American War had been fought in her absence. Uncle Teddy's Rough Riders had made him so popular that he was chosen Vice President, becoming President after McKinley was assassinated in 1901. Uncle Teddy's niece spent an unhappy time in New York with her Aunt Pussie, who was just emerging from a broken love affair and took out her chagrin on Eleanor.

"You are so homely, no one will ever want to marry you," she screamed. When Eleanor remained silent, her aunt scathingly announced that Eleanor's father had been an alcoholic.

Sobbing, Eleanor begged her grandmother to assure her this was false, but the latter gravely confirmed the tale. Elliott Roosevelt's drinking had ruined her mother's life, she told Eleanor. He had spent his last years in a private sanitarium.

Radiantly beautiful on her wedding day, she wore a white satin dress covered with rose-point lace and a veil fastened with a diamond crescent which had belonged to her mother.

Temporarily, America seemed a hateful place, and she pleaded to return to Allenswood. For once her grandmother let her have her wish, but only for a year. At eighteen she must be home for her debut in New York society.

As was the custom, her name was put on Social Register lists for debutante parties. Night after night her maid escorted her to the ballrooms where these affairs were held. Eleanor in her pretty French gowns was as shy and ill at ease as when she was fourteen. She stood the social whirl for about a year and then refused to continue. The dances bored and exhausted her.

Charity — with a capital "C" — was a permissible outlet for young debutantes. For the Consumers League, which was investigating sweatshops, she visited slum homes where whole families, even children of four or five, worked at making artificial feathers and flowers until they dropped of fatigue. She also joined the newly formed Junior League, for which her activity was to teach "calisthenics and fancy dancing" at the Rivington Street Settlement House.

Sometimes Franklin Roosevelt, now in Harvard, dropped by the settlement house to take her home. Once a little girl fell ill, and Eleanor asked him to carry the child to her parents. It was his first sight of a New York slum and he blanched. "Gosh, I didn't know anyone lived like that," he told Eleanor.

Gradually he began squiring her around to plays or to dinner or simply for long walks. She enjoyed his friendship but it did not occur to her that his intentions were serious. She still thought herself unattractive though in fact she had become quite pretty, tall and willowy with soft blond hair, smooth skin, and expressive blue eyes. Moreover, Franklin found her much more interesting than most of the girls he met. In the fall of 1903, he proposed to her. Flattered, and certainly incredulous, she accepted.

"Are you sure you are really in love?" demanded Grandmother Hall when Eleanor confided her engagement.

"Yes," she said solemnly.

They were married in New York City on March 17, 1905. She was twenty and Franklin not quite three years older. All the important New York socialites attended the wedding, and Uncle Teddy came up from Washington to give the bride away. Immediately after the ceremony he congratulated the young couple and hurried into the library. The guests followed the wedding's star attraction, leaving the newlyweds alone.

Franklin looked at her and grinned. "Well, we might as well join the party," he said, taking her arm.

They were a serious young couple, who talked much about books and social welfare, but now and then they indulged in a bit of horseplay too.

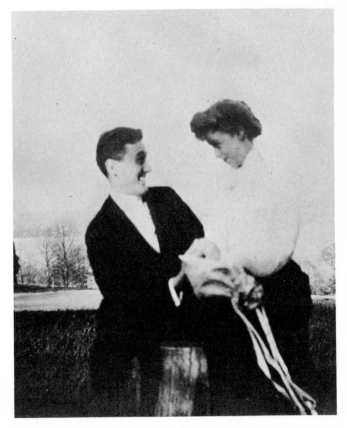

II. America in Peace and War

"Human relationships, like life itself, can never remain static."

Their honeymoon was postponed three months, so Franklin could continue his law studies at Columbia University. The delay made them appreciate all the more their three months in Europe. Never before or afterwards were they so carefree.

The proprietor of Brown's Hotel, in London, under the impression that their reservation was for the United States President, installed them in the luxurious Royal Suite. It was far beyond their means, but they stayed on several days for the thrill of it.

In Paris, they dined in tiny restaurants and strolled along the river Seine, browsing at the book stalls where Franklin made endless purchases for his library. It pleased Eleanor to find that he spoke fluent French. He bought her some lovely clothes, including a pastel blue afternoon dress and a white net evening gown and cloak, and one night he took her to the Follies, which rather shocked her.

They visited Italy, rode in a gondola in Venice as she had done in her childhood, ordered blown glass with the Roosevelt crest in Murano, toured through Germany and the Swiss Alps, returned to France, then settled in England for the rest of their holiday.

One evening they had dinner with Sidney and Beatrice Webb, founders of the Fabian Society and England's leading authorities on social problems. It amused Eleanor afterward to remember that she spent the evening discussing the servant problem with Mrs. Webb, while her husband explained Harvard's educational policy to their erudite host.

For a while they stayed with Lord Ronald Ferguson, former Governor-General of Australia. At tea, Lady Ferguson asked Eleanor to explain the relationship between the American federal government and the states. The niece of the Presi-

The young married couple in Italy.

The honeymooners. Franklin was photographer for this picture of his young wife. Sitting in a Venetian gondola, she held his straw hat and pretended to be absorbed in a newspaper.

[23]

dent had never given this subject a thought and was saved from disgrace only because Franklin walked in.

"Darling, Lady Helen would like to know the relationship between the federal government and the states."

He took over from there, as she knew he would, but she resolved never again to be caught in such an embarrassing situation.

Back in New York, she adapted herself to the pattern "of a fairly conventional, quiet young society woman," more than a little under the domination of her mother-in-law. Mrs. Sara Roosevelt, who had hated to lose her only son, now took his marriage under her wing. She had rented a house for them, complete with servants, on East 36th Street. Later she built two adjoining houses on East 65th, one for herself, the other for her son and his wife.

In face of such overwhelming generosity, Eleanor was defenseless. Nearly every afternoon she went driving with her mother-in-law. Sara usually ate at least once a day with them. They spent weekends at her beautiful home in Hyde Park, and in the summer they all went up to Campobello, the lovely island off Maine where Franklin had always spent his vacations.

He took a job with a New York law firm but was not too happy about it. Their first child arrived in May, 1906, a blond-haired girl they named Anna Eleanor after her mother. James was born in December, 1907. Sara persuaded Eleanor to hire a nurse to look after them. She later admitted this was a mistake. Most of the nurses who invaded Eleanor's home in the next years not only bossed her around but on occasion punished her children so unjustly that she had to order them out.

In time Sara's influence over Eleanor waned. For all her good qualities she belonged to a hidebound aristocracy whose thinking was cast in iron molds: servants must not be spoiled; the "lower classes" must be kept in their place. As Franklin and Eleanor became increasingly concerned with the rights of the common people, the gulf between them and this dynamic old lady widened until no true communication was possible. But they always loved her dearly.

An inexplicable restlessness pervaded Eleanor those early years of her marriage. She enjoyed playing with her children and being in the company of her husband, but she still had energy left over. She did an enormous amount of embroidery and knitting and read nearly every popular novel and biography. She took up golf because Franklin liked it, but was so awkward that he gently advised her to try another sport. When they bought an early model Ford in 1908, she decided to learn to drive but gave up after running into a gatepost.

Her third child lived only a few months. For a long time she was morbidly unhappy, convinced that somehow she was to blame. Not until the next September, in 1910, after Elliott was born, did her pain begin to ease.

Franklin entered politics in 1910, with a zest he had never shown for law, and was elected State Senator from Duchess County on the Democratic ticket. They moved to Albany, where Eleanor's task was to play hostess to his political colleagues, a rough-and-tumble lot on the whole. She rather liked the bluff, cigar-smoking Al Smith — though her mother-in-law distinctly disapproved of him — but she was most unfavorably impressed with a gnomelike, wizened, incredibly untidy little newspaperman named Louis Howe. Howe admired Franklin because of his courageous stand against the bosses of the corrupt Tammany Hall and soon began calling him, only half jokingly, "most revered future President."

[25]

Franklin Roosevelt's birthplace at Hyde Park overlooking the Hudson River. Much later it would be a National Historic Site.

Frances Perkins, Boston-born social worker who became America's first woman Cabinet member.

The tragic fire of the Triangle Shirtwaist Factory in 1911 focused attention on the wretched working conditions of factory women employees.

On March 25, 1911, the Triangle Shirtwaist Factory in New York City caught fire and nearly a hundred and fifty working girls perished in the blaze. It took this shocking tragedy to expose the sweatshop conditions which Eleanor and her friends had investigated back in 1903. An elegant young woman from Boston named Frances Perkins helped organize women in a crusade for fire prevention. Subsequently, Miss Perkins came to Albany to lobby for a fifty-four-hour work week for women. Eleanor and Franklin met her at this time. Miss Perkins considered Eleanor a quiet housewife and thought Franklin an "arrogant fellow." In time she changed her opinion of both of them.

That year Franklin took his wife to Baltimore where she attended her first Democratic presidential convention. He was campaigning for Governor Woodrow Wilson of New Jersey, a former professor who believed that the government should be taken from the hands of the few and entrusted to the many. For Eleanor, the hot and noisy meetings were unbearable, and she soon left to take the children to Campobello. It was there that she received a joyous telegram from her husband, telling her that Wilson had been nominated.

In March, 1913, Franklin went to Washington to attend President Wilson's inauguration, and while there was appointed assistant to the Secretary of the Navy, Josephus Daniels. Eleanor was pleased because he was. The whole family moved to Washington, as did Louis Howe, who had become her husband's political adviser.

The wife of the Assistant Secretary of the Navy had certain duties required by protocol. On Mondays, she called on the wives of the Justices of the Supreme Court. On Tuesdays, she left cards with the congressmen's wives, and on Wednesdays, the wives of Cabinet members. Thursdays were devoted to senators' wives, and she paid her respects to the wives of diplomats on Fridays. Her cousin, Mrs. Alice Longworth, the daughter of Uncle Teddy, thought calling on women a waste of time, but to Eleanor this was heresy. If the tedious routine helped her husband, it was her duty.

The Franklin Roosevelts became one of the most popular young couples in Washington. Women found Franklin extraordinarily handsome, and everyone liked his pleasant, smiling wife. They had friends their own age and some older ones, such as the learned Justice Oliver Wendell Holmes. On Sunday evenings they held open house, and Eleanor, dispensing with servants, made scrambled eggs on a chafing dish, her only culinary accomplishment.

Two more sons were added to their family during their Washington stay, Franklin Delano, Jr., in August, 1914, and John, born in March, 1916. Anna and her four brothers were all handsome children. With her old sense of inferiority, Eleanor rejoiced that they took after their father, not herself. She read them Kipling's *Jungle Book*, Ernest Thompson Seton's *Wild Animals I Have Known*, and James Barrie's play, *Peter Pan*, which the enchanting actress, Maude Adams, had immortalized.

In the meantime war had broken out in Europe. Franklin, certain that the United States would be involved sooner or later, stepped up his efforts to build America a strong Navy. At first

A complete family. Franklin and Eleanor Roosevelt in 1916 with their five children (left to right), Elliott, Franklin Delano, Jr., James, John, and Anna Eleanor.

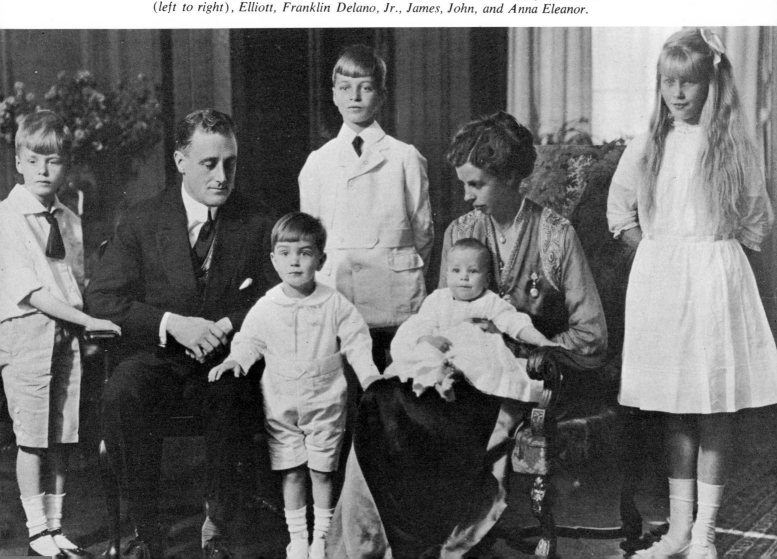

Eleanor was inclined to agree with Secretary of State William Jennings Bryan, who dramatized his pacifist beliefs by presenting government officials with miniature plowshares made from old guns. The German torpedoing of the *Lusitania,* with its civilian cargo of men, women, and children, changed her mind. She could not forgive this act of treachery.

Nor could President Wilson, who wanted peace more than anything else, hold out against Germany's continued acts of aggression. Eleanor attended Congress on April 2, 1917, the day he asked for a declaration of war on Germany.

Almost overnight, so it seemed, the young men of the nation appeared in uniform. Women who had never worked before took jobs in war industries. "Give until it hurts" became the nationwide motto, as Liberty Bond rallies swept the country. From a gay social place, Washington turned grim. Calling on government officials' wives was out for the duration. Eleanor was soon loaded with war activities.

With Mrs. Josephus Daniels, she helped to organize the Navy League, which distributed free wool to be made into sweaters for the "soldier boys" overseas. Like other women, she carried her knitting everywhere.

Several days a week she reported to a Red Cross canteen, an iron shack in the Washington railroad yards where, in temperatures often over a hundred degrees, she scrubbed floors, washed dishes, made coffee and sandwiches for trainloads of men on their way "over there." Once she cut her finger almost to the bone, but as it was a busy day she wrapped a handkerchief tightly over the wound and went on making sandwiches. The doctor later took several stitches, and the scar always remained.

Regularly she visited the naval hospital, bringing flowers and delicacies to the wounded, and once she stopped by St. Elizabeth's Hospital for the Insane, where the Navy had taken over wards for shellshock victims, youths whose minds had cracked in stress of battle. The military patients

The "Yanks" in Paris. Victory Parade down the Champs-Élysées, November, 1918.

were receiving adequate care, but she was horrified at the way the civilian patients were neglected. With courage born of her indignation, she called on the Secretary of the Interior, demanding that something be done for them. Eventually, as the result of her efforts, an increased appropriation was made, and St. Elizabeth's became a model institution of its kind. For the first time in her life she had shown her ability to "get things done."

Often she had to rush home from the canteen to preside over a formal dinner for some English or French official visitors. Since time was of the essence, she learned to "dress with rapidity," a habit she retained.

Franklin took a European inspection tour in July, 1918. On the return trip he caught pneumonia. Eleanor, on instructions from the Navy, met his boat with a doctor and an ambulance. She nursed him in New York and Hyde Park. It was the middle of October before he was well enough to resume his duties in Washington.

The influenza epidemic had arrived in full force there. Franklin had a relapse, and all five children and three servants were soon down with the "flu." Elliott developed double pneumonia. Luckily Eleanor found a trained nurse, and with her help they all recovered.

In the overcrowded city, there were not enough hospitals to take care of the sick. The Red Cross set up temporary installations, often in buildings without kitchens. In addition to caring for her own invalids, Eleanor volunteered to prepare food for patients in a women's shelter. She distributed it herself, going from cot to cot, and speaking comfortingly to the lonely young girls lying there.

The epidemic had barely subsided when, on November 11, 1918, the Armistice was signed. Washington, like every other city, went wild. There were bells ringing, parades, whistles blowing, and people throwing confetti all day long.

All over America, women set up canteens for their soldiers and sailors, like this one in Kansas.

Throughout America, in cities and on farms, wives and mothers made preparations to receive their returning heroes.

One side effect of the war was to raise the stature of women in public opinion. The long campaign of the suffragettes was at last bearing fruit. Eleanor learned what was in the offing from a senator's wife whom she met on a train to Washington. An amendment to give women the right to vote was before Congress, the senator's wife confided. Perhaps influenced by her husband, she wanted Eleanor to take a public stand against its ratification. Eleanor, usually so docile with her elders, refused to commit herself.

She herself had never had any desire to vote but on the other hand she could think of no good reason why women should not vote if they wished. She had to think about it more before she made up her mind one way or another.

Very soon thereafter the nineteenth amendment passed Congress. "The right of citizens of the United States to vote shall not be denied or abridged by the United States or by any State on account of sex," it said. The date was August 26, 1920.

III. Time of Crisis

*"Every time you meet a crisis and live through it,
you make it simpler for the next time."*

In the summer of 1921, the whole family was united on their island home at Campobello. For Franklin, it was a long postponed and well deserved vacation. After the war, he had taken Eleanor to Europe, where he had official business to finish. They returned on the same ship with President Wilson, who had succeeded in making the League of Nations part of the Versailles Treaty, and was now preparing to sell America on the idea. When subsequently James Cox and Franklin Roosevelt became Democratic candidates for President and Vice President respectively, the chief plank in their platform was Wilson's League of Nations. They were defeated overwhelmingly by the Republicans. The American people did not want the League of Nations or any other "foreign entanglement." Warren Harding of Ohio was now in the White House.

It was a grave setback, but Franklin did not allow himself to be discouraged. "There will always be a next time," he said cheerfully, and settled down to a few weeks of relaxation with Eleanor and their children.

Then, on August 10, at the end of a marvelous day of camping, sailing, and swimming, came tragedy. Eleanor's strong, healthy, athletic husband was stricken with infantile paralysis. Happily for all of them, they did not yet guess that he would never walk again.

There followed weeks of excruciating pain, as with iron determination, he gritted his teeth and forced himself to exercise the injured muscles. As the months went by, he taught himself to crawl, to pull himself up a flight of stairs, to use crutches, and to stand erect with the aid of heavy steel braces. Swimming in the mineral waters at Warm Springs, Georgia, did much to restore his health, but contrary to his hopes it did not cure him. The proud young aristocrat became humble, feeling himself one with suffering humanity. He invited

President and Mrs. Woodrow Wilson. Wilson succeeded in making the League of Nations part of the Versailles Treaty, but could not persuade America to join the League.

American and Canadian flags fly from the double flagpole at Campobello.

*To restore her husband's interest in politics, Eleanor held meetings of Democrats
at her New York home on East 65th Street. Louis Howe is seated on her right.
Henry Morgenthau, Sr., stands at her left between Nancy Cook and Caroline O'Day.*

other polio victims to share Warm Springs with him and started the Warm Springs Foundation for Infantile Paralysis, which became a national institution.

In this, the first serious crisis of her life, Eleanor came through magnificently. This was no time for hysterics. Added to everything else, there were the children, terrified at what had happened to their father, who must be reassured.

She was always close to her daughter, except for one brief period in adolescence. The younger boys were interested in outdoor sports which their father could no longer share with them. She saw that unless she became a more "all round" person, she would lose them. She resumed riding horseback, made herself learn to swim, took a long camping trip with her sons, and, after a couple of minor mishaps became quite a good driver. The one thing she could never bring herself to do was to discipline her offspring. She left that to their father, who invariably found excuses not to.

Her other most important job was to keep up her husband's morale. No one knew better than she the bitterness and the discouragement behind the cheerful mask he assumed for others. Louis Howe, who had joined them in Campobello after the catastrophe, became at once her adviser and her comrade. Her early antagonism to this odd little man vanished before his solicitude. After Franklin was brought home from the hospital,

Howe came to live with them in New York, sacrificing his own family life, everything, for the man whom he still called by that ridiculous title, "revered future President."

Together Eleanor and Howe defied Mrs. Sara Roosevelt, who wanted her son to stay at Hyde Park in retirement. Eleanor was sure Franklin would die a slow death if Sara had her way. He loved people, loved being in the thick of things. She felt he must resume his political interests. But how could it be arranged?

"You can do it, Eleanor," Howe told her.

"What do you mean?"

"You must go into politics. That will rekindle his interest."

She was aghast. "I would not know how to begin."

"You can do it."

How did he know? How did he guess that this shy young matron was good for anything but managing her home? It had not occurred to Franklin, though he loved her dearly and appreciated her intelligence. It took this cynical ex-newspaperman to see qualities in her no one else had suspected, with the possible exception of Mlle. Souvestre of the Allenswood school.

Howe was unimpressed with her work for the League of Women Voters, a tedious assignment she had taken on of analyzing legislation, but he was pleased when she was invited to a lunch of the Women's Trade Union League.

The WTUL was founded in 1904 at a time when female factory help worked eighteen hours a day, and laundry workers had to iron a shirt a minute, standing in a steam-filled room on burning hot cement floors. Eleanor, with her very different background, listened with anguish, and fascination too, to the women's stories of their bitter struggles to better their lot. She joined the League as an associate member and made good friends

Albany newspaperman Louis Howe launched Eleanor Roosevelt into politics and dedicated his life to her husband's career.

there, particularly with Maude Schwartz, who had done her apprenticeship in a British printers' union, and with little red-haired Rose Schneiderman, an organizer for the garment workers.

"Bring them home," proposed Louis Howe.

The women came, reluctantly at first, and then freely, as they discovered that the Roosevelts for all their money had nothing snobbish about them. As for Franklin, their visits were a tonic. He laughed heartily at Maude's funny stories, and had long discussions with Rose about the history of the labor movement.

At Christmas Eleanor arranged for Franklin Jr. and John to give a party for the children of the League members at their clubhouse, over Sara's protests they would catch some dreadful disease. About twenty-five children came. Franklin read Dickens' *Christmas Carol* to them, as he always did to his own brood. It was a huge success.

Through two friends, Marion Dickerman and

Nancy Cook, Eleanor joined the Women's Division of the Democratic Committee. Because of the prestige of the Roosevelt name, they asked her to speak at a fund-raising luncheon. She was absolutely terrified and had no idea what she said, but she raised $12,000 and soon was pressed to speak elsewhere.

Howe slipped in once and listened from a back seat. Later he criticized her cruelly. "Why did you giggle? There wasn't anything funny." She did not know she had. "Don't do it again," he told her. "Keep this in mind. Have something to say. Say it and then sit down!"

It was years before she felt herself adequate as a public speaker, though she proved to be an excellent campaigner.

With a fellow member, Caroline O'Day, she called on a Democratic leader to ask him to add more women to his local group. The man's wife told them he was out. Somehow Eleanor was not convinced.

"We'll wait on the porch until he comes home," she said cheerily.

Two hours later, the door opened and the man came out of hiding from the "female politicians." "You win," he said sourly.

Eleanor laughed, explained their mission, and won his consent.

When she was assigned to edit the Women's Division paper, Louis Howe taught her how to proofread and prepare headlines. She needed no help on the writing, which came far easier to her than making speeches.

She took Howe's criticism, which was often harsh, without resentment, feeling that his efforts were for the thing they both wanted most — a full life for her husband. Howe's plan was working. More and more political friends, men as well as women, were coming to their house. Franklin was taking an active part in their discussions.

His public re-entry in politics was at New York City's Madison Square Garden, when he mounted the stand with the aid of seventeen-year-old James, and nominated Governor Al Smith as Democratic candidate for President. The "Happy Warrior," he called Al, and the delegates cheered wildly, not especially for Governor Smith, who did not win the nomination, but for Franklin Delano Roosevelt, who had come back.

On a plot of farmland about two miles from the Hyde Park mansion, Eleanor had a cottage built so she could entertain her own friends without imposing on her mother-in-law. There, with Nancy Cook and Marion Dickerman, she started a small non-profit factory, called Val-Kill, where unemployed young men of the community were trained to make reproductions of Early American furniture. Franklin did not participate but called it "a grand idea."

The next year the three women purchased the exclusive Todhunter School in New York City. Henceforth, three days a week, Eleanor taught the girls American history and literature and gave a civics course she called "Happenings," which included field trips to courtrooms, police line-ups, and slums. She wanted her students to know what was going on outside of their fashionable homes.

In this period of the "Roaring Twenties," when young women were flaunting their independence with knee-length skirts and bobbed hair, Eleanor shortened her dresses only a few inches and still wore her long blond hair coiled around her head. In appearance, if not in her thinking, she was noticeably old-fashioned.

A number of women made headlines in this decade. There was Joan of Arc, who in 1920, was canonized a saint by Pope Benedict XV, four centuries after her martyrdom. There was night club owner, Texas Guinan, inventor of the phrase, "butter-and-egg man." Marie Curie, the first woman to be awarded a Nobel Prize, ventured across the Atlantic in 1921, escorted by her two daughters, Eve and Irène, to receive in a much publicized White House ceremony a gift from the women of America of a gram of radium — worth about a hundred thousand dollars.

Gertrude Ederle, a New Yorker, swam the English Channel in 14 hours and 31 minutes, in 1926, the first woman to accomplish this feat. In the same year, MGM starred an unknown Swedish actress of extraordinary beauty and talent named Greta Garbo, in a picture called *The Torrent*. And on May 22, 1927, Mrs. Evangeline Lindbergh, a Detroit schoolteacher, received a call from her son Charles in Paris over the new transatlantic phone, telling her what the world already knew — that the first air flight across the Atlantic had been successfully accomplished in 34 hours, 20 minutes, and 30 seconds.

Little more than a year later, June 17, 1928, a pretty and daring young pilot, Amelia Earhart, became the first woman to cross the Atlantic by plane.

"Amelia has promised to give me flying lessons," Eleanor told her husband.

For once he put his foot down. "What are you trying to do to me?" he demanded. "You know I have enough worries on my mind without worrying about your flying around up there somewhere in the sky."

In January, 1929, the Franklin Roosevelts moved back to Albany, this time to occupy the Executive Mansion. The four years that Eleanor spent as the wife of the Governor of New York marked both a continuation and an expansion of her previous activities. She joined the new Junior Literary Guild as a member of the editorial board, reading and judging books for teen-age girls. She wrote magazine articles, spoke over the radio, went on teaching at Todhunter, be-

Eleanor Roosevelt examines the work of a young employee of the Val-Kill furniture factory.

Marie Curie, the world's most famous woman scientist, gave the name "radioactivity" to a phenomenon first noted by Henri Becquerel, and, with her husband, Pierre Curie, discovered two radioactive elements — polonium and radium.

To help depression victims, she had her own program. To beggars who accosted her in New York streets, she gave a printed card saying they could receive free meals at the Roosevelt home. Once she kept a young hobo overnight there, to the consternation of her family. In Albany, word spread around that anyone could get help by applying to the Governor's wife. Photographs of her began to appear frequently in the papers and were nearly all unflattering. "The camera misses her freshness, charm, and intelligence," wrote one reporter.

Amelia Earhart, the first woman to cross the Atlantic by plane, later made solo flights across the Atlantic and across the Pacific from Honolulu to California. Her plane was lost in the Pacific in 1937 during her attempt to fly around the world.

came editor of a magazine called *Babies, Just Babies.*

She began to earn a good deal of money on her own, which she spent to pay off a mortgage on the Women's Trade Union League clubhouse and to set up two recreation halls where unemployed girls could have lunch, rest, and mend and press their clothes while looking for work. This was during the depression which descended on America, and on a good part of the world, after the stock market crash of October, 1929.

The Governor took her with him on a tour of state prisons and hospitals for which he believed additional appropriations were in order. Since he could not walk, she went inside to inspect conditions. The first time this happened, she told him what was on the patients' menu.

"Did you make sure they were actually getting that food?" he asked. She admitted she had not.

Soon she was looking in pots on the stove, opening closet doors to see if folding cots were stacked away, inspecting every nook and corner. As her powers of observation increased, she was seldom misled by external appearances.

She acted frequently as her husband's proxy, laid cornerstones, attended flower shows, opened bridges, went to state and local fairs. Sometimes she made speeches for him.

Politics had become a habit with her, and she continued her work with the Democratic Party because she enjoyed it and because it seemed worth while. She backed Frances Perkins as chairman of the State Department of Labor, and continually promoted women's interests. Even before her husband felt it politically wise, she spoke out for state unemployment compensation.

When her husband became presidential candidate in 1932, she would not campaign openly for him but did what she could behind the scenes. On election day, she and Franklin voted in Hyde Park, then went to New York to await the returns. It was not until two o'clock in the morning that Herbert Hoover conceded the election. Shortly thereafter two strangers entered the room. Eleanor asked them who they were.

"Secret Service men," they said. "Our job is to guard the President."

Among the guests at Governor Roosevelt's Inaugural Ball in Albany were (left to right) Al Smith and Mrs. Smith, Herbert Lehman, and Mrs. Sara Roosevelt.

At his first inauguration, March 4, 1933, President Roosevelt addressed a nation plunged in a fog of despair. "We must act and act quickly," he said, "... the only thing we have to fear is fear itself."

IV. The Roosevelts in the White House

"Courage is more exhilarating than fear and in the long run it is easier."

Inauguration Day — March 4, 1933 — dawned damp and dreary. Eleanor, sitting with the children in the inaugural stand at the Capitol, watched with pride and concern as her husband, supported by their oldest, James, walked along the red-carpeted ramp to take his oath of office. She sensed a mood of helpless despair among the spectators.

The four-year-old depression had mounted the ranks of the unemployed to fifteen million, and the specters of hunger and want stalked the land of the free and the home of the brave. Yet the people, bewildered as children at the disaster which had befallen them, had chosen as their leader a man who could not walk unaided. "It was," she wrote later, "a little terrifying."

Then she heard his voice, clear, cheerful, resonant. "Let me assert my firm belief that the only thing we have to fear is fear itself." The tension of the crowd seemed to ease, almost as though by these few words her husband had passed along the same courage with which he faced adversity.

Across the seas, Nazi Chancellor Adolf Hitler, just two months in office, was launching his campaign against the Jews and plotting mass arrests of anti-Nazis. Mussolini was at the height of his popularity, as he promised the people to restore Italy to its ancient glory and as a first step decreed that the Roman salute should replace the handshake. At Geneva, the League of Nations unanimously — and futilely — condemned the unprovoked Japanese invasion of Manchuria.

In her feminine world, Eleanor approached with something like awe her duties as mistress

The President and First Lady, fulfilling their duties as ordinary citizens, vote at Hyde Park in the New York State election.

of the White House, which had sheltered American Presidents since John and Abigail Adams moved there in 1800 — when water still had to be brought a distance of several city blocks. Thomas Jefferson, who preferred his dream house, Monticello, called the White House big enough "for two emperors, one Pope, and the Grand Lama." Under the glittering chandeliers of the East Room, Abraham Lincoln had rested in his black-shrouded bier in April of 1865. And in 1886, in the Blue Room, big Grover Cleveland had married Frances Folsom, the first and only presidential marriage in the White House.

Never, throughout her stay, did Eleanor lose the feeling that she was surrounded by the shadows of the past. Once she looked up from her desk and was certain she saw Lincoln pass her window.

Sistie and Buzzie Dall, her grandchildren, enjoy their swing on the White House lawn.

She was impatient as always in a new place to get settled, and on the practical side there was much to be done. The Monday following the inauguration, she and her housekeeper, Mrs. Henrietta Nesbitt, a former Hyde Park neighbor, explored their new home from cellar to attic.

Mrs. Nesbitt was overwhelmed at the thought of supervising the large White House staff, of keeping sixty rooms in pristine order, and of planning meals for the President of the United States and his unknown quantity of guests.

"You're not to worry about anything," Eleanor reassured her, patting her on the shoulder. "You're going to be all right."

Presently the First Lady was helping the servants move the furniture around. Ike Hoover, Chief Usher of the White House for some forty years, reproved her gently.

"That isn't done, Mrs. Roosevelt."

Not he nor anyone else could change her ways.

The rooms on public display must retain their formal elegance, but there were no rules against making their own quarters more livable. In the upstairs Monroe Room, she replaced fragile antiques with solid Val-Kill reproductions which would withstand the horseplay of her boisterous sons, and across from the portraits of President Monroe and his wife she hung an oil painting of her grandfather, Theodore Roosevelt, after whom her Uncle Teddy was named. In her husband's bedroom she installed an extra-length Val-Kill four-poster bed, and finding her own bedroom too large for her taste, she converted it into a study and had her bed moved into the small dressing room. She plastered her husband's prints of sailing ships all over the walls and even in closets.

She demanded that a swing be hung from a tree on the White House lawn for her grandchildren, Buzzie and Sistie Dall. The maintenance chief, Colonel Ulysses S. Grant III (grandson of

The First Lady in the Monroe Room of the White House, beneath the portrait of her grandfather, Theodore Roosevelt, Sr.

another United States President), argued that the swing would injure the tree.

"Really, Colonel," she told him firmly, "I've always had rope swings swung over branches, and they never hurt the bark."

She found that servants off duty had nowhere to go but the gloomy basement. A first item on her agenda was to have their quarters made cheerful and pleasant. "Oh, I don't know what we would do here without Mrs. Roosevelt," said one of the maids later. Eleanor wanted to do something about the old-fashioned kitchen, which was hardly sanitary, but the household allowance did not stretch that far. Not until 1936 was she able to have it modernized. She could and did dispense with cuspidors and provided the servants with modern cleaning equipment to replace outmoded and ineffective feather dusters and corn brooms.

At her desk in the White House, she confers with her regular secretary, Malvina Thompson, and Mrs. Edith Helm, her social secretary.

Franklin's political opponents had been jeering derisively at her multifarious activities, one paper gleefully prophesying that Eleanor Roosevelt was sure to wreck the administration. Though she could not see she had done wrong, she was resolved to keep out of the political limelight, lest her husband suffer for it.

Night after night the experts whom Louis Howe dubbed the "Brain Trust" conferred with the President, planning the New Deal measures designed to bring prosperity back to the nation. Eleanor wandered around restlessly. "I could not go to bed out of personal curiosity to know what was being done," she confessed.

Howe's ambition was realized. He no longer need say "revered *future* President." Even so, he was not willing to let Eleanor Roosevelt retreat into the background. "You must hold press conferences for women reporters," he informed her blandly.

Half-heartedly, she protested that as First Lady she was not to meddle in public affairs. A pity, he commented. Reporters were being fired left and right these days. The hatchet always fell first on the women. Her press conferences might have saved some of their jobs. She yielded at once.

Her first press conference, held in the Red Room on March 6, 1933, was not a total success. There was a certain awkwardness on both sides, and even the box of candy she passed around failed to relieve the strain. Nonetheless, a beginning had been made and a precedent shattered. With time a strong bond grew between the President's wife and the women of the press.

Later that year, she entertained women reporters at the Gridiron Widows dinner, on the same night that newspapermen held their stag Gridiron Club affair. This became an annual function and was always fun. Once, at a masquerade, the First Lady disguised herself as "Apple Annie" in shawl and bonnet. When she uncovered her face, the shrieks of laughter resounded throughout the White House.

From Albany she had brought her personal secretary, Malvina Thompson, better known as "Tommy." Together they handled the mass of letters addressed to the First Lady. They were mostly requests for money, jobs, or intervention with some government agency. Whenever they sounded reasonable, Eleanor did what she could. She became a one-woman employment agency. Many of her correspondents received a personal check from her, with no questions asked. To one nine-year-old lad she sent the banjo he wanted more than anything else in the world.

Their first formal White House dinner was for Ignace Paderewski, pianist-composer and Premier of Poland. Guests were served roast beef with mint jelly, green peas, pan-roast potatoes, and strawberry ice cream. Mrs. Nesbitt recalled ruefully Theodore Roosevelt's dinner in 1902 for Prince Henry of Prussia which took a three-page menu to list all the fancy dishes. But this was the depression and it seemed improper to Eleanor that they should feast while others went hungry. For the same reason she served the Cabinet ladies a soup of spinach and dandelion greens for lunch. There was such a stir that she never repeated the experiment.

Matters of protocol she left to her social secretary, Edith Helm. Mrs. Helm kept a list of diplomatic functions, handled invitations, and consulted the State Department about who should sit next to whom, a White House regulation that Eleanor resented though eventually she understood the necessity for it. It seemed equally senseless, besides being exhausting, to invite a thousand guests to tea, until she realized how much the occasion meant to them.

To the established annual affairs, she added

A WPA artist gives finishing touches to a mural.

several of her own: parties for the National League of Women Voters, for her former students at Todhunter School, and for handicapped children. Most shocking to her critics, she entertained some young girls from a reformatory. Often she invited one of her many protégés to a dinner

Eleanor Roosevelt with Mrs. Mary McLeod Bethune, Director of Negro Affairs of the NYA. Mrs. Louis S. Weiss at right.

of notables — a Chinese student, a member of a youth movement, a comparatively unknown writer whose book had pleased her. Her reason: "I thought it would be interesting for them."

The actress, Eva Le Gallienne, came to lunch and talked of the need of a government-sponsored theatre. The Works Project Administration, set up to create jobs for the unemployed, was getting under way. Eleanor persuaded Harry Hopkins, the WPA director, to include a Federal Theatre Project for unemployed actors and playwrights. WPA theatres were presently cropping up from coast to coast. The people loved them, but there were storms of protest over the extravagance of it.

The WPA Artists Project, the Federal Writers Project, other projects for unemployed dancers and musicians, all were partly the result of her enthusiasm. She also sponsored a WPA project for seamstresses, who made garments, bed covers, and mattresses from surplus cloth, serving the dual purpose of helping the destitute and giving jobs to older women. Nothing escaped scathing comments about how the government was wasting the taxpayers' money.

Of all the depression victims, Eleanor was most troubled about the youth. "A stranded generation," she called these boys and girls who could not afford to continue their education and who had no place to go, nothing to do. To Harry Hopkins and his deputy administrator, Aubrey Williams, she proposed that projects be started for teenagers, to supplement the CCC camps. When they were convinced, she broached her idea to her husband, being careful to point out that this too might bring criticism. People might say that American youth was being regimented like Hitler youth.

"If it is the right thing to do for the young people, then it should be done," he said. "I guess we can stand the criticism."

With the lightning speed in which everything was achieved in those days, the National Youth Administration came into being. It gave high school and college students a chance to finish school, to learn a trade, to work on a part-time basis. Unlike the CCC, it was open to girls as well as boys. It was designed for all young people, regardless of race, creed, or color. The NYA Director was Aubrey Williams, and the Director of Negro Affairs was Mary McLeod Bethune, the first member of her large family to be born out of slavery and the first Negro woman to hold such a high government post.

The expected criticism never came. From the beginning the NYA was an enormous success. NYA projects were set up in schools in every part of the country. The First Lady never missed an opportunity to visit one of them, however small. The NYA was her brainchild and she was justly proud of it.

Though Louis Howe had steered her back into public activity, she now had to do without his advice. They had given him the Lincoln Room at the White House, an honor that failed to impress him since he considered F.D.R. the greatest American President, barring none. His health began to fail in 1934, and for months he was confined to his bed. Eventually he was taken to the hospital where he died in April, 1936. For both Franklin and Eleanor he was irreplaceable.

The WPA and NYA were temporary agencies. This was not true of the Social Security Act, passed by Congress on August 14, 1935, the fruit of Franklin Roosevelt's conviction that the government was responsible for the well-being of its people. The act provided old age and unemployment insurance, aid to needy elderly persons and to the blind. There was as yet no provision for agricultural workers or household servants. That would come later.

THE ROOSEVELTS IN THE WHITE HOUSE

Child labor, as abhorrent to the President as to his wife, received its first substantial federal blow in the minimum age standards of the Walsh-Healey Act in 1936. More comprehensive legislation to protect children was included in the Fair Labor Standards Act two years later.

During the 1936 presidential campaign, Eleanor accompanied her husband for part of his western tour. There were those who said that the country was being "run to blazes" in the name of Roosevelt, but they were a minority. The depression was receding, and millions gave Roosevelt credit. There was no need to sit up late waiting for election results. He won by the biggest landslide vote in history.

Roosevelt adored the excitement of a political campaign, and his wife shared his enthusiasm. They are shown here on a whistle-stop tour with their youngest son, John, and Miss Anne Lindsay Clark.

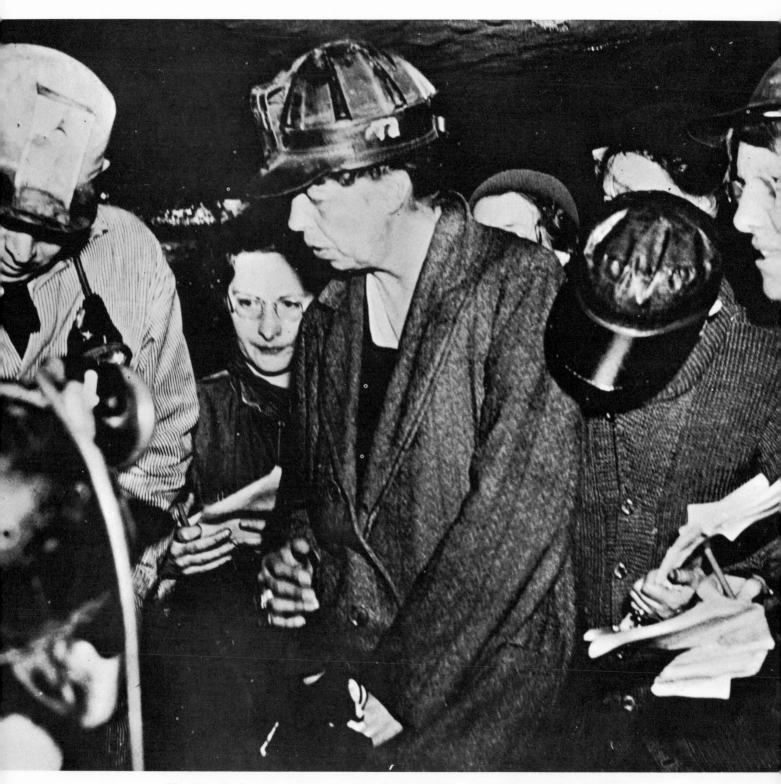

The First Lady wanted to see for herself the working conditions of the coal miners of Bellaire, Ohio, and insisted on going down into the pit. Still wearing her miner's helmet, she discusses her reactions with the mine superintendent.

V. Ambassador to the Common People

*"I never can understand why so many people are afraid
to live their own lives as they themselves think is right."*

Parallel to her home activities, Eleanor acted as her husband's special investigator and ambassador to the American people.

It began in the spring of 1933 when, feeling the need of a brief change, she took a motor trip through Quebec and Maine with her friend Lorena Hickok, of the Associated Press. On her return, the President questioned her closely about how people lived in Maine, what their farms were like, how the Indians were getting on. From then on she became his eyes and ears in all the places he could not visit himself.

From the Quakers she learned that the miners of West Virginia were in desperate circumstances. In the fall she went to this mining region and found people living on scraps, sleeping on rags in houses not fit for habitation. Whole families were ill with typhoid, as the result of a contaminated water supply. There were men who had been on relief for five years, and there were working miners who, after the company deductions were taken from their pay, received less than a dollar in cash each week.

She returned with wealthy friends, whom she led from shanty to shanty until, gasping, they offered her whatever she wanted if only she would not make them look at any more misery. Financier Bernard Baruch helped her establish a school,

and with the help of Mrs. Leonard Elmhurst she set up a children's clinic. For a long time her own earnings from radio and writing went to her West Virginia miners. Over the years she visited them repeatedly, gave them advice on starting small farms, attended their church socials and barn dances, became an adopted mother to them.

In 1934, at her husband's suggestion, she went to Puerto Rico where conditions were even more shocking than in West Virginia. The work for the sugar companies was seasonal and wages pitifully small. In between, there was near starvation. In city slums she saw huts made of bits of

*For one large Puerto Rican family, this wretched
shack was home.*

tin and scrap iron and wood. She would never forget the little girls in their school lunch hour embroidering handkerchiefs to add a few pennies to the family income. She went on to the Virgin Islands, where conditions were only slightly better. On her return she begged her husband to send labor experts and industrialists to find ways to remedy the situation. Some of her friends later started small industries there.

Also at Franklin's request, she inspected some federal prisons, a painful chore, for she could hardly bear to see people shut up. Once she left early to go to a Baltimore prison and did not have a chance to remind him of her mission. Later in the day he asked Tommy where she was.

"In prison," Miss Thompson told him dryly.

"I'm not surprised," he said. "But what for?"

During his first two terms in office Eleanor averaged thousands of miles a year. She went down into the coal mines of Ohio. She visited the farmers in the Midwest Dust Bowl, the migratory

Mrs. Roosevelt presents the Spingarm Medal to contralto Marian Anderson. The medal is given each year to an outstanding American Negro.

Children at a migratory workers' camp in California are delighted to find that the President's wife is paying them a visit.

workers in California, the sharecroppers of the South, and Washington's own slum area. An Indian tribe gave her the name of "Ow-du-sees-ul," meaning, "Princess of Many Trails."

In the South she saw the signs "colored" and "white" above drinking fountains. To her this was "un-American" and she said so, over and over, year after year. Her most highly publicized blow against discrimination was her resignation from the Daughters of the American Revolution after the DAR refused to let Marian Anderson sing in Washington's Constitution Hall. But she did not put all the blame on the South. "We are wrong in many ways in the North," she told an audience in Atlanta, Georgia.

Beginning in January, 1936, she wrote a daily newspaper column she called *My Day*. Within two years it was being syndicated to 140 papers across the country. Usually she dictated it to Tommy, then corrected the rough draft. She wrote it on planes, on ships, in a moving automobile, and, once, on a destroyer.

Following the 1936 election campaign, she went on her first lecture tour. Wherever she spoke she urged women to take advantage of their right to vote and participate actively in their government. She and Lillian Wald, founder of New York's Henry Street Settlement, did their best to get James Farley, now Postmaster General, to issue a stamp honoring women. He would not go that far, but subsequently he appointed some four thousand women to jobs in post offices. Some claimed she was responsible for the appointment of Frances Perkins as Secretary of Labor, the first U.S. woman Cabinet member, but she denied it.

Mrs. Roosevelt at the airport in Kansas City, Mo., September, 1932.

She approached gruff Hugh Johnson, Administrator of the National Recovery Act, to ask that the NRA codes include a clause granting women equal pay with men for the same work. He told her that to do so would be contrary to the American pattern. "It's time you changed the American pattern," she said, and he had no further argument. Unfortunately the victory was temporary. The NRA was one of the New Deal casualties, declared unconstitutional by the Supreme Court.

She bombarded the Secretary of the Interior, Harold Ickes, with memos about the plight of the Indians, and telephoned Henry Wallace, Secretary of Agriculture, asking him to send surplus pigs to her West Virginia miners. As a result of her persistence, the President set up the Federal Surplus Commodity Corporation, to purchase farm surpluses and pass them on to relief agencies. She forgot, or at least ignored, her early resolution to stay out of things. When something needed to be done, and she could do it, it seemed to her she had no choice.

She was an active member of the National Conference on the Cause and Cure of War, founded by Carrie Chapman Catt, and so extreme in her pacifism that she would not give toy guns and soldiers to her children. "The war idea is obsolete," the First Lady said in 1935, the year that Mussolini invaded Ethiopia. Her remark would later be tossed back at her with a vengeance.

In Nazi Germany, trade unions were banned and with them all rights of organized labor. Only Nazi professors were allowed to teach the young; books not in accord with Nazi ideology were burned. As for women, every gain they had won in the past decades was revoked. The place for women, said Hitler, was in the kitchen — which would have aroused Eleanor's antagonism even if he had done nothing else.

Thousands of German citizens, including schol-

[49]

ars and scientists of international reputation, fled their native country or were forced into exile because of their Jewish birth or their anti-Nazi ideas. Many came to America, seeking freedom from oppression as their European ancestors had done many years before.

When Hitler occupied Czechoslovakia in 1939, Eleanor denounced Germany as "a sinister power with no scruples" and advised sending military planes to France. Joseph Goebbels, Hitler's propaganda chief, blasted out, "It is not good for a nation when the wife enters the political china shop," and Mussolini, who had a certain wit, called for an "embargo on Eleanor Roosevelt." Thus did she enter the international scene.

The year 1939 was a busy one socially at the White House. A total of 4,729 people came to lunch or dinner, and 23,267 attended teas and receptions. The rooms open to the public were seen by 1,320,300. There were 323 house guests. The parents and children who attended the annual Easter egg-rolling contest totaled 53,108; one hundred and eighty of the children were lost — and found again.

No guests received so much publicity as did King George VI and Queen Elizabeth, who arrived in the spring at the invitation of the President.

Beforehand, Ambassador Bullitt in Paris sent a secret memorandum, listing in infinite detail what the royal visitors would require for their comfort. It amused Eleanor greatly that he specified soap and towels in the bathrooms. Would anyone have done less for any guest? Nonetheless a flurry of housekeeping preceded their visit. The Red Room and the Blue Room were completely redecorated, and new wall-to-wall carpets were laid in the Rose Room, which was to be occupied by the Queen.

It was a pleasant relief, after all the turmoil, to find that the King and Queen were a friendly

No matter how many things she had to do, Eleanor Roosevelt rarely missed the annual Easter egg-rolling contest, the one White House festivity planned solely for children.

The First Lady talks with the Queen while President Roosevelt exchanges a jest with King George VI. Roosevelt supports himself on the arm of Brigadier General Edwin M. Watson.

and undemanding couple. The Queen endeared herself to Eleanor permanently by praising her for attending a WPA union meeting, an incident that had evoked a particularly virulent attack on her. There were, however, a few conflicts between the White House staff and the royal servants. An usher made the mistake of asking the Queen's maid to give a message to the lady-in-waiting. She told him, haughtily, that it was not her place to do so.

The usher looked at her in disgust. "Oh, so you're a big shot!" he commented.

At Hyde Park the King and Queen were later given a taste of characteristic American food, including a picnic, where hot dogs were served among other dishes, and entertainment was provided by American Indians.

The Roosevelts took their guests to their train at the Hyde Park station. As Eleanor waved them good-by her heart was heavy with pity, thinking how dreadful it must be to know that one's country might soon be faced with the terrible ravages of war.

She was in Hyde Park again in September, three months after the departure of England's royal couple. At five in the morning her husband called her. The Germans had marched into Poland, he said. He did not need to tell her any more. The war had started in earnest, and there was little chance that any part of the world could escape it.

Adolf Hitler's Mein Kampf, *published in 1924, outlined his plan for world conquest. By 1940, his fantastic ambition seemed well on the way to becoming a reality.*

VI. World Conflagration

*"Within all of us there are two sides. One reaches for the stars,
the other descends to the level of beasts."*

The New York World's Fair, where sixty participating countries displayed their art and culture, gave a pleasant respite from thoughts of war. Eleanor visited it a number of times in 1939 and 1940, officially and unofficially, and always enjoyed herself. Particularly she liked to dine on the terrace of the French restaurant, watching the fountains change as vari-colored lights played on them.

She had taken an apartment in New York, thinking that soon their tenure at the White House would be over. Repeatedly, she was asked whether her husband would be a candidate for an unprecedented third term. She, no more than anyone else, could give an answer. For his own sake, she hoped he would not, yet she knew that there was no one to take his place in this time of crisis. It was not until the early summer of 1940, shortly after the Nazi blitzkrieg invasion of western Europe, that Franklin agreed not to refuse the nomination.

Neither of them planned to attend the 1940 Democratic National Convention in Chicago, but in the midst of it Eleanor received a frantic call from James Farley. All was not well, he told her. There was no doubt about Roosevelt being nominated, but many were reluctant to accept Henry Wallace, his choice as Vice Presidential candidate. Things were in a mess. Would Eleanor fly out and talk to them?

She agreed, reluctantly, for again it would be setting a precedent. No First Lady had ever addressed a presidential convention. The hall, dim with cigar smoke, was in pandemonium when she arrived. There was so much booing it was impossible to tell who was objecting to what. As she headed for the speaker's stand, she held herself tall and proud, as she always did when she wished to hide her own fears. But there was no hesitation in her speech. Gently and firmly, she reminded the delegates of their duty:

New York World's Fair.

Mrs. Roosevelt talks with United States Paratroopers, somewhere in England, on her wartime visit there.

[55]

The First Lady gives a warm welcome to royal refugees from war-torn Europe — Princess Juliana, heiress to the Netherlands throne, and her husband, Prince Bernhard.

"We cannot tell from day to day what may come...We shall have to rise above considerations which are narrow and partisan. This is a time when it is the United States we fight for."

As she resumed her seat, the organist played "God Bless America." The convention proceeded in an orderly manner. Henry Wallace was chosen Vice Presidential candidate, as Roosevelt had wished.

Mrs. Roosevelt with Mayor Fiorello LaGuardia.

"You did a very good job, Babs," he told her afterwards.

Royal refugees began arriving at the White House, among them the Grand Duchess of Luxembourg and Crown Princess Juliana of Holland. As before, there were other house guests, musicians, artists, explorers, motion picture stars. Carl Sandburg came and strummed on his guitar for them. Alexander Woollcott, who had inspired the play, "The Man Who Came to Dinner," made the White House his headquarters whenever he was in Washington. "It's the best theatrical boarding house in town," he told Ethel Barrymore. Flippant as Woollcott often was, his admiration for the First Lady was genuine. "Mrs. Roosevelt is the greatest woman alive and if she came into this room, we all ought to get down on our knees before her," he once burst out to Booth Tarkington.

The President spent less and less time with their guests and more time in private conferences. In August, 1941, he told his wife he was going fishing up the Cape Cod Canal. Much later she learned he had met with Prime Minister Winston Churchill off the coast of Newfoundland.

The next month an Office of Civilian Defense was set up, with fiery little Mayor Fiorello LaGuardia of New York as director. Eleanor became deputy director. She worked long hours without pay, and it proved a thankless undertaking. Her theory was that community projects should be established to teach people to work together should the need for home defense arise. LaGuardia tended to think of defense in terms of more of the fire engines he adored. When Eleanor appointed Mayris Chaney, a dancer, to head a recreational program for children, a storm arose. "One might have thought Congress considered dancing immoral," she commented sadly.

The news of the Japanese bombing of Pearl Harbor, December 7, 1941, stunned her as it

More important visitors came to the White House in the next month, including the presidents of Bolivia, of Czechoslovakia, and of Liberia; Prime Minister Mackenzie King of Canada, and Madame Chiang Kai-shek, wife of the Chinese Generalissimo, who brought with her a retinue of forty persons.

"How do you manage to travel with only your secretary?" she asked wonderingly. "Who packs your bags?"

"Why, I pack mine, and Tommy packs hers," Eleanor told her.

So well had Eleanor done her job in England that early in 1943 her husband decided to let her

P/Sgt. Vincent J. Buffamonte, a wounded U. S. Marine in a South Pacific military hospital, is visibly cheered by a visit from Eleanor Roosevelt.

tour the South Pacific. She agreed at once, stipulating only that she must visit Guadalcanal, which had been taken at such fearful cost. At first he objected that it would be too dangerous, but he finally gave her a letter to Admiral William Halsey saying she could go there "if it did not interfere with the conduct of the war."

Since she was an official representative of the Red Cross on this trip, she wore a Red Cross uniform, which simplified the matter of luggage. In all, she traveled over 23,000 miles. In Australia, where she spent eleven days, she followed the men along jungle trails, noting how they had been trained to stand motionless, to detect an enemy and yet remain unseen. She was eight days in New Zealand, where she voyaged either in a lumbering train or an army jeep.

Admiral Halsey, whom she met at Noumea, stalled her as long as he could on the Guadalcanal trip but eventually yielded, finding Mrs. Roosevelt a woman who could not be discouraged once she had made up her mind. She visited sixteen other islands as well. The amazement of the men at these lonely outposts, finding that the First Lady had come to see them, has been described many times. Whenever she could manage it, she took mess with the enlisted men rather than with the officers, sometimes getting up before six to share their breakfast.

She visited hospitals and more hospitals, including one where each patient was allotted one cup of water a day, for both drinking and washing. There is no record of how many miles of wards she walked, but once she visited the wounded in fifty-two wards after fourteen hours of travel. She was gone five weeks and lost thirty pounds. Though she felt a little tired when she got home, the doctor could find nothing wrong with her health.

While Eleanor was away that spring of 1943, North Africa was cleared of Axis forces in the first major Allied offensive of the war. In the enslaved countries of Europe, both men and women were fighting their oppressors in the growing Resistance movement. April 19 marked the start of the terrible battle of the Warsaw Ghetto. Jews and Resistance fighters alike were being herded into concentration camps, where millions died of starvation or in gas chambers. On the Eastern front, Stalingrad had withstood the Nazi siege, and the Soviets were on the offensive.

In America, from Pearl Harbor Day to March, 1944, six and a half million women entered the labor force for the first time, working as welders, truck drivers, riveters, railroad sectionmen, or enlisting in the WAACS, WAVES, and SPARS. Anna Rosenberg, a tiny, soft-voiced woman, was made Assistant Secretary of Defense. Illinois, Massachusetts, New York, and Washington became the first four states to pass laws for equal pay for men and women on the same jobs.

The First Lady went on one more long wartime trip in March, 1944, a 13,000-mile tour of the Caribbean area and South America. In her absence, and with all their sons in service, the President found the White House a lonely place and sent a plaintive letter to a friend:

"My Missus is in Recife, Brazil; Anna is in Boston; Jimmy is in Hawaii; Elliott is in a camp near London; Franklin, Jr. is at the Miami camp, and Johnny is on an aircraft carrier headed out."

In January, 1945, after the American people had chosen him for a fourth term of office, Franklin Roosevelt went to Yalta in the Crimea for a second meeting of the "Big Three" — himself, Winston Churchill, and the Soviet leader, Josef Stalin. It was over six months since the D-day invasion. The end was in sight. The major point on their agenda was setting up a plan Roosevelt had conceived, a United Nations to carry on where the League of Nations had left off.

The long trip exhausted him. Seeing how haggard he looked, Eleanor persuaded him to go to Warm Springs for a needed rest. His two cousins, Margaret Suckley and Laura Delano, accompanied him, and Eleanor telephoned daily. But on April 12, Laura Delano telephoned her. Franklin had fainted, she said. They had put him to bed and called the local doctor.

On the advice of her husband's regular physician, Dr. Ross McIntyre, Eleanor kept her afternoon appointment, a benefit concert for the Thrift Shop, at the Sulgrave Club. While she was there, she was called to the telephone. It was Steve

Early, the White House press secretary, who asked her to come home. She did not need to ask why.

He and Dr. McIntyre were waiting for her. A hemorrhage, they told her. The President had died without recovering consciousness. It was the most terrible moment of her life. Yet shortly afterwards, when Vice President Harry Truman arrived, she told him the news calmly.

"What can I do?" he asked, choking.

"Tell us what *we* can do," she said gently. "Is there any way we can help you?" She realized, if he did not, that he was now the President of the United States.

To her four sons, she cabled: "Father slept away. He would expect you to carry on and finish your jobs."

With Steve Early and Dr. McIntyre, she took a plane that night for Warm Springs. It was not yet dawn when they reached the cottage known as the "Little White House." Leaving the two men, she walked inside without a word. She wanted to be alone with her husband for one last time.

President Roosevelt at the Yalta Conference, with Secretary of State Edward Stettinius and Soviet Premier Stalin. The strain of twelve years in office, during the crisis of the depression and the catastrophe of the war, has noticeably aged him.

[61]

VII. United Nations at Work

"Anyone who really hopes for ultimate disarmament knows that it cannot happen unless we have a strong UN."

Eleanor wanted to get away from the memory-filled White House as fast as she could. Within a week after her husband's death, she had packed and sorted a thirteen-year accumulation of household goods and fled. In those first days over a hundred thousand people wrote their sympathy for her loss. For once, she could not answer them personally but let President Truman pass on her gratitude at a press conference.

She refused his invitation to attend the San Francisco Conference on the United Nations Charter, which opened April 25, 1945. Thousands urged her to run for President or Vice President; she pointed out to them that the country was not yet ready for a woman chief executive. Nor would she run for the Senate: "I want to be able to say exactly what I please and to feel free."

Since 1944, the Roosevelts' Hyde Park home had been designated a national historic site. While Eleanor still had the right to live there, she preferred her nearby cottage, Val-Kill. She also kept her apartment on Washington Square, in New York City, where she spent the first terrible weeks of her widowhood.

The war against the Nazis was marching to its dramatic finale. On April 13, the day after President Roosevelt's death, American troops liberated the notorious concentration camp of Buchenwald. The equally infamous Dachau, in Bavaria, was liberated April 29. On this day a tall, gray-haired woman in black made her first public appearance since the loss of her husband, at the dedication of the new 45,000-ton aircraft carrier, the *Franklin D. Roosevelt*.

Mrs. Roosevelt speaks at the launching of the aircraft carrier, the Franklin D. Roosevelt, *at the Brooklyn Navy Yard, April 29, 1945 — her first public appearance since her husband's death.*

Nuclear power was first used as a weapon of war when a bomb was dropped over Hiroshima on August 6, 1945. A second atom bomb fell on Nagasaki on August 9. The great mushroom cloud has become a symbol of man's capability for total destruction.

It was not her nature to sit home and feel sorry for herself. Soon she was taking up all her old causes and some new ones. Roosevelt's dog Fala was to be returned to Margaret Suckley, the Scotty's original owner, but James Roosevelt asked her to let his mother keep Fala. "She has no one living whom she is personally responsible for," he said. He underestimated his mother.

At Rheims, France, Germany signed an unconditional surrender on May 7, a few days after Adolf Hitler apparently committed suicide in the rubble of Berlin. In the Pacific the conflict dragged on three months longer. To bring it to a halt, President Truman authorized use of atomic bombs — on Hiroshima, August 6; on Nagasaki three days later. The Japanese surrendered August 14.

In New York, the National Broadcasting Company arranged a long-distance telephone interview between the Austrian refugee scientist, Lise Meitner, in Sweden, and Mrs. Roosevelt. Miss Meitner, when in exile, had deduced that certain neutron bombardment experiments of her Berlin colleagues were causing the atom to split — a discovery that led to America's vast atomic energy project. Mrs. Roosevelt spoke to her before they went on the air and found she was panic-stricken with stage fright.

"Don't be afraid," Mrs. Roosevelt told her. "Listen very carefully to what I say and then answer slowly...You really speak English very well."

The Austrian scientist followed her advice and the broadcast succeeded.

In December, 1945, President Truman appointed Eleanor Roosevelt as delegate to the United Nations General Assembly in London. The "cold war" was already looming. In view of the universal love for Truman's predecessor, it seemed a wise move to have a Roosevelt in the United States delegation. Eleanor accepted with trepidation, feeling she lacked experience. Unknown to her, some members of the Senate had vigorously but vainly opposed her appointment.

The American UN delegation was seen off on the *Queen Elizabeth* on New Year's Eve by a horde of reporters and newsreel cameramen. Mrs. Roosevelt was busy up to the last moment and arrived when the fanfare was over. A customs man saw her hurrying toward the gangplank unescorted. "Mrs. Roosevelt!" he burst out in shocked surprise. "May I help you?"

A panoramic view of Hiroshima after the bombing. In early 1945 Hiroshima was a prosperous Japanese city of some 334,600 population. The bomb — a tiny one by later standards — laid waste about 60 per cent of the buildings, killed nearly 100,000 persons, and seriously injured another 100,000.

On shipboard she announced to her colleagues that she wished to take part in the daily briefings and discussions. So well did she grasp the complicated issues, and so much did she contribute to these meetings, that by the time they landed in Southampton she had won the grudging admiration even of those members who had most strongly objected to her presence.

England had not forgotten her courageous wartime visit. Crowds blocked traffic around her hotel, cheering every time she appeared. She had lunch with the King and Queen but left immediately

afterwards, apologizing on the grounds that she had so much work to do.

The UN Assembly opened formally on January 10, at Central Hall, London. Delegates from fifty-one member nations were present, with Belgium Prime Minister Paul Henry Spaak acting as president. In an atmosphere of cigar smoke, not unlike that of the Democratic conventions, the Assembly elected the Norwegian, Trygve Lie, as UN Secretary-General, set up the Security Council, the Economic and Social Council, the International Court of Justice, the Atomic Energy Commission, and other working committees. Mrs. Roosevelt was assigned to the Social, Humanitarian, and Cultural Committee, possibly because that seemed the safest place for a woman.

From the beginning the sessions were heated, and again and again she played the role of peacemaker. Although she was the only woman in the U.S. delegation, there were a number of women connected with delegations from other countries. She invited them all to her hotel to tea, thinking it might help if the women at least

Lise Meitner, forced to flee Nazi Germany in 1939 because of her Jewish birth, played a major role in the development of nuclear energy.

Mrs. Roosevelt with Queen Mary, mother of King George VI.

talked over the problems of their countries informally. Sixteen came the first time, including a Russian woman delegate with her interpreter. This was the prelude to many dinners and parties Eleanor gave for UN delegates, men and women, who not only became her friends but closer friends with America through her efforts.

An immediate concern of the UN was the plight of some 30,000,000 European children left homeless by the war. UNICEF, the UN International Children's Emergency Fund, was set up as a temporary agency to care for them. Mrs. Roosevelt found homes for many of the children and personally took over the support of some twenty of these young victims of a war they had not made. Because of her work in this field, UNICEF gave her the title of "Friend of the World's Children."

Under the jurisdiction of the Social, Humanitarian, and Cultural Committee was the problem of the displaced persons still in Germany, particularly Poles, Czechoslovaks, Lithuanians, and Estonians. The position of the United States was that these refugees should have the right to choose whether or not they went back to their homes. The Soviet Union contended that many of them were Nazi collaborators who should be returned to their countries of origin and, if the situation warranted it, brought to trial.

The Committee discussions grew so taut that eventually the matter was brought before the Assembly proper. Andrei Vishinsky, Soviet Union Foreign Minister, defended the Russian view. Largely due to Mrs. Roosevelt's forceful support of the American position, Vishinsky was defeated.

"I hope the day will come when you and I are on the same side of a dispute, for I admire your fighting qualities," she told him later.

"And I, yours," Vishinsky replied promptly.

While she was undergoing her apprenticeship with the United Nations, world-wide attention was centered on a great drama being enacted at the

As guests of UNICEF, these three little Polish girls eat a warm and nourishing meal. UNICEF gave supplementary aid to some 700,000 needy women and children of Poland, one of the twenty-four war-impoverished countries they served.

Palace of Justice, in Nuremberg, Germany. This was the trial of twenty-one major war criminals of Nazi Germany by the First International Military Tribunal, conducted by eight judges, two each from France, England, the United States, and the Soviet Union. From November, 1945, to September, 1946, the prosecution unrolled its gruesome evidence of Nazi brutality and lawlessness. By the verdict, eleven of the defendants were sentenced to death, seven received prison terms, and three were acquitted. For the first time in history, makers of aggressive wars were brought to trial by the countries against whom they had warred, setting a precedent for the future.

At the close of the London UN sessions, Mrs. Roosevelt flew to Germany, where she had her first look at its shattered cities, the price the German people had paid for their loyalty to Der Führer. While there, she visited several refugee camps, including one for Jewish persons at

In London, Mrs. Roosevelt meets two old friends, Sir Winston Churchill and his wife, Lady Churchill.

Zilcheim, made up of wretched barracks which housed several families in one room.

One day an old woman knelt before her in the muddy road, crying out in despairing tones, "Israel! Israel!"

Mrs. Roosevelt was deeply moved, aware for the first time of the yearning of this woman and others like her for a country of their own. Later she vigorously fought for more American aid to Israel, and kept after President Truman until the United States recognized the Israel Government in May, 1948.

She thought that now her work with the UN was ended, but soon after her return to New York, she was called to serve on the Human Rights Commission of the UN General Assembly. The meetings opened October 23, 1946, in temporary quarters at Lake Success, Flushing, Long Island. Untiring, she worked a strenuous six-day week, ate in the crowded cafeteria with the other employees, and carried her own laden brief case. It was generally agreed that she was the most popular and the most effective member. She was certainly one of the busiest. A staff officer was as-

Nuremberg Trial. The 21 defendants, accused by the Allied nations of the most hideous crimes in world history, sit resignedly in the prisoners' dock at Nuremberg. Field Marshal Hermann Goering, second in command to Hitler up to the last few days of the war, slouches on bench lower left.

signed to assist each delegate. She was given two assistants, since one alone could not keep up with the pace she set.

The task of the Human Rights Commission, of which she became chairman, was to formulate a Universal Declaration of Human Rights. This seemingly simple assignment was fraught with incredible difficulties. "Human rights" meant different things to countries in various stages of economic and social development. A poor country like India was not ready to guarantee secondary and higher education to the young. Moslem countries were doubtful about the article guaranteeing religious freedom. Countries where women were still kept in subjection, without property rights or other privileges, hesitated to accept a drastic change.

The discussions, which dragged on interminably, were continued in Geneva, Switzerland, in December, 1947; and in Paris, when the UN met there in 1948. By this time Mrs. Roosevelt had become a master of parliamentary rules of order.

She opposed the tactics of the Soviet delegates, whom she felt devoted far too much time and energy criticizing American "imperialism." The Russian delegate, Dr. Alexei P. Pavlov, speaking about Negroes in America, once claimed that workers were dying of starvation in California by the thousands. Mrs. Roosevelt called an American Negro educator to testify that this charge was false.

Another day, the Soviet delegate charged that Mississippi had a law forbidding any man to strike a woman with an axe handle — that is, if the handle was more than two feet long. To Mrs. Roosevelt's considerable embarrassment, her researcher discovered there was indeed such a law still on the statute books of that state.

In 1948 she returned to London for a moving ceremony — the unveiling of a ten-foot statue of

Mrs. Roosevelt, accompanied by King George VI, attends the unveiling of her husband's statue in Grosvenor Square, London. The sculptor, Sir William Reid Dick, depicted Roosevelt as a vigorous young man, standing erect.

Franklin Roosevelt in Grosvenor Square. The King and Queen were at her side during the unveiling, and she stayed with them at Windsor Castle. Princess Margaret, like many an American teenager, played popular records for her friends. Princess Elizabeth, on the other hand, had become a serious young woman; she engaged Mrs. Roosevelt in a discussion about the value of a certain British rehabilitation project for women offenders.

The final vote for the Declaration of Human Rights was cast after midnight in Paris, on December 10, 1948, with several countries still abstaining. It was, people said later, Eleanor Roosevelt's greatest triumph. For the first time in history, the world had a document clearly stating the things to which everyone should be entitled.

"All human beings are born free and equal in dignity and rights," it read. By its articles all had the right to life, liberty, and security of person; to a fair and public hearing in a court; to freedom of thought, of assembly, of religion, of the press; the right to social security, to an adequate standard of living, to an education, and to take part in the cultural life of one's country.

Because it specified that these rights should belong to all, with no distinction as to sex, this document became considered as the greatest step forward of the twentieth century in women's struggle for equality.

There was nothing legally binding in the Declaration as yet. Mrs. Roosevelt continued her work with the UN four years more, chiefly on the covenants by which member nations would obligate themselves to carry it out. It was to influence the constitutions of Costa Rica, Libya, Indonesia, and other countries, and had a role in the Japanese peace treaty.

In 1952, New Jersey became the thirteenth American state to enact an equal pay law for men and women. Korea was transformed into a bloody battleground, where young Americans were among those who gave their lives. George VI, who had long been ailing, died quietly in his sleep. Princess Elizabeth was in East Africa with her husband, the Duke of Edinburgh, when she learned that she was Queen of England.

In New York, the year 1952 marked the completion of "UN-Ville," the group of dazzling modern buildings on the East River which were the permanent home of the United Nations. No longer was it a dream of the future but a reality of the present, which in spite of numerous crises and some bitter criticism had proved itself worthy of its name. The least publicized of its activities were perhaps the specialized agencies devoted to eradicating poverty, disease, and ignorance in undeveloped areas: the World Health Organization, the Food and Agriculture Organization, UNICEF, now helping underprivileged children the world over, as well as UNESCO, the UN Educational, Scientific, and Cultural Organization.

In step with the humanitarian agencies of the UN was the United States Four Point program, an outgrowth of President Truman's foreign aid bill of 1948, which was helping other countries to develop their own agricultural and industrial resources, providing food for the hungry and medical care for the sick, as well as schools and teachers for the young.

It must have pleased Mrs. Roosevelt to see these concerted, if still insufficient, steps toward the "good neighborliness" between nations which her husband had always advocated.

When Dwight D. Eisenhower was elected Republican President in 1952, she sent in her resignation from the UN. She had served a good part of the last seven years in this great cause, and it seemed to her that she could now let others take over.

VIII. Far Distant Places

"Do not stop thinking of life as an adventure."

As a child she had dreamed of going to "far distant places" with her father. All the traveling she had done thus far had not quenched her zest for adventure. In her sixty-eighth year, at an age when most have retired from active life, she began her longest and most varied voyages.

Prime Minister Nehru had once invited her to visit India. In 1952 she decided to accept his offer and at the same time to see some of the other countries about which her UN friends had aroused her curiosity. She took only two companions with her, Maureen Corr, who was substituting as her secretary, and her personal physician, Dr. David Gurewitsch.

At the suggestion of Dr. Charles Malik of Lebanon, with whom she had worked on the Human Rights Commission, she stopped first in his native land, where she was fascinated by the hills patterned with tiny farm plots interspersed with archeological excavations of an ancient civilization. Evidently the government expected some display of public hostility because of her support of Israel; a lorry of soldiers accompanied her wherever she went until she said bluntly that she did not need them nor want them.

She visited briefly two other Arab countries, Syria and Jordan, drank bitter black coffee in the home of a workman in Damascus, talked with all sorts of people, including the dictator of Syria, toured camps of Palestinian refugees from Israel which were distressing and depressing beyond description.

Next there were seven days in Israel, a new country with buildings going up everywhere, new health clinics, schools, agricultural projects, farmers trying to make the desert bloom where there had been desolation before. She was aware that

This youthful citizen of Israel, paralyzed as the result of an attack of polio, was provided treatment through the World Health Organization (WHO). Not yet cured, he is able to feed himself with the aid of an arm sling.

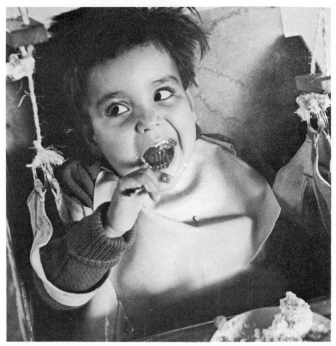

At the magnificent Somnathpur Temple in Mysore, India. With Mrs. Roosevelt are her Indian hosts, her physician, Dr. David Gurewitsch (at her right) and Maureen Corr (behind her).

[71]

Still wearing the wreaths presented to her on her arrival in India, Eleanor Roosevelt stops to chat with girl students of a village school.

many problems were still unsolved, but her feeling was strong that these were a pioneer people dedicated to a noble purpose.

Her next port of call was Pakistan, which like India since 1947 had been an autonomous dominion within the British Commonwealth. She had known and admired the Pakistan leader, Liaquat Ali Khan, at the UN; he had guided the country until his assassination in October, 1951. Now his wife, the Begum Liaquat Ali Khan, was doing a splendid job in encouraging women to take a role in civil affairs.

When Mrs. Roosevelt's plane brought her down to the Karachi airport, she was greeted by a vast sea of women in uniform, the Begum's All Pakistan Women's Association. They loaded her down with wreaths of flowers and long chains of gold tinsel around her neck. On the slow drive into town, the road was lined with children waving American and Pakistani flags and shouting, *"Pakistan Zindabad! Mrs. Roosevelt Zindabad!"* "Long live Pakistan! Long live Mrs. Roosevelt!"

During her stay she learned more of the difficulties of transforming the status of women overnight. She saw some women on the street still wearing *burkas,* hot, heavy capes which covered them completely except for a slit for their eyes. Although they had the right to vote, many were timid about doing so. Every time she addressed a women's group, she told them about the early struggles of the League of Women Voters in their efforts to educate women to their new responsibilities, thinking that the example of American women might serve as an inspiration to them. In Lahore, she attended a *purdah* party, where men were not admitted. After supper the young women danced and sang their native songs for her. In turn, to Pakistani music, she taught them the Virginia Reel.

At the time of the partition, Pakistan Hindus and Sikhs had gone to India, while thousands of Indian Moslems had crowded into Pakistan. Many of them lived in open camps, and it was not unusual to see barbers or cobblers plying their

It takes skill to master the technique of this ancient Indian spinning wheel.

This fearless Nigerian lad watches with curiosity as a WHO doctor gives him an injection.

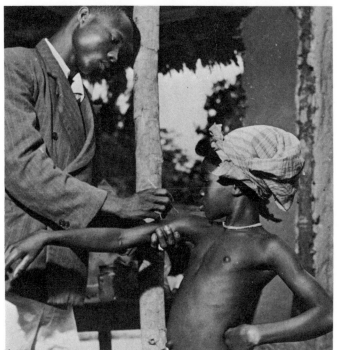

trade on the sidewalks. At a refugee settlement for these unfortunates she saw children drinking milk furnished by UNICEF — a word which some children now believed to be American for "cow."

Before she left she visited a jute factory, watched a splendid exhibition of Arab horses, lectured to young men and women students at the University of Peshawar, and, as a grand climax, visited the great shale and limestone cliffs of the Khyber Pass, which had impressed her father over seventy years before.

Prime Minister Nehru and his famous sister, Madame Pandit, were at the airport of New Delhi to welcome her to India. The next morning she placed a wreath on the funeral pyre of Mahatma Gandhi, who, by peaceful means, had done more than anyone else to gain India independence. Far in advance of his time and his people, he treated women as equals, claiming indeed that they were morally superior to men. Because of his influence, the new Indian government had been able to find capable women for high posts in considerably larger ratio than in the United States.

From New Delhi she left on an air trip that would take her to many far corners of this vast

India's Prime Minister Nehru and his sister, Madame Vijaya Lakshmi Pandit, entertain Mrs. Roosevelt at a reception in her honor in their New Delhi home. Cabinet ministers, military personnel, and other top-ranking officials attended.

and mysterious country. One day she joined a group of white-robed villagers, sitting cross-legged as they did, while they talked to her of their need, not for charity but for seed and fertilizer for their fields. Again, she attended a formal reception in Bombay in linen dress and tennis shoes — because she had no time to change and thought it rude to be late. At Nehru's request, she addressed the Indian Parliament. She learned to greet her new Indian friends in the Indian manner by the *namaskar,* folding her hands before her and bowing her head.

In Bombay also, she attended a class in reading and writing for slum women, given in the home of one of them. A merchant learned she was coming and presented her hostesses with a bolt of white China silk. By the time she arrived it had been unrolled all the way up the rickety stairs for her to walk on.

At Trivandrum, the southwest tip of India, she rode up the canal in a motorboat among fishing craft with huge nets hanging from the masts, while multitudes of ragged children, obviously suffering from malnutrition, stood watching from the shores. In Mysore, she was taken to see the Chamundi Temple and the great sculptured Chamundi Bull. Her escorts told her if one crawled beneath the arched front leg of the bull and made a wish, it would come true. It was not beneath her dignity to do so.

She reached Hyderabad in time for the ancient Holi carnival, during which people gathered on the streets and threw bright dyes at each other, coloring their hair, skin, and clothes. She visited the Ellora Caves, temples hewn out of solid rock by eighth century Buddhist monks; the Ajanta caves, some of which dated back to the third century, and at last the Taj Mahal, the most beautiful building in the world, which she saw at dusk, by moonlight, and in the morning when the rising sun turned the white marble to rose.

There was a quick air trip to the tiny kingdom of Nepal on the slopes of the Himalayas. Mrs. Roosevelt was back in Calcutta to attend the opening of the United States Information Service library, where Indian citizens could now come to read books and magazines about life in America. On her last night in India she talked at length with Nehru, as to a friendly big brother, telling him where she had been, what she had seen, and what were her reactions.

She spent a few days in Indonesia, where she ·dined with President and Mrs. Sukarno, then she was off across the Pacific to the Philippines. The plane passed over Bataan and Corregidor, names which brought back a sad page of American history, bringing her down to Manila. There, she had a private audience with President Querino, spoke to a large group of government officials and delegates from women's organizations, and visited a village for orphans whose parents had been killed in the war. She made stops at Guam, Wake, and Honolulu on her way to San Francisco. By the time she reached Hyde Park at the end of this fabulous journey, she had been away

Buddhist monks in Cambodia learn about life in the United States through USIA publications.

five months. *India and the Awakening East,* a book about all she had learned in her travels, was published the next year. No one could say how she found time to write it.

Her next long trip was to Japan in the spring of 1953. She had been invited there to explain to Japanese women, who were just emerging from long feudalism, the manner in which a democracy functions. With the same simple courtesy she had shown elsewhere, she went about making friends with the citizens of the country that had been responsible for Pearl Harbor. She conferred with college presidents and labor leaders, and in any number of cities gave lectures to groups of women in all stations of life.

An interview with Emperor Hirohito and his wife, the Empress Nagako, was arranged for her. This was considered to be a special privilege, even for the widow of President Franklin D. Roosevelt. Beforehand, she was coached as to what she should wear, how she should bow, how she should enter the room and leave it. Obligingly she followed all the old customs but one. Breaking the rule that no one should speak to the royal couple unless they spoke first, she told them of what the women in Pakistan and India were doing to liberate themselves from the tradition of slavery. As she certainly expected, the Empress was intensely interested. Their unprecedented discussion lasted an hour.

Before she left Japan, she made a pilgrimage to Hiroshima, the first city to know the horror of nuclear warfare. No experience had ever so saddened her. "God grant to men greater wisdom in the future," she said.

She returned homeward by the western route, stopping at Hong Kong, Greece, and Turkey. She visited Yugoslavia, touring farms and factories and spending a day with President Tito at his island home at Brioni. In between their quite serious discussions about his country's economic

In Japan. Mrs. Roosevelt visits an ancient temple in the village of Nikko, Honshu, largest of Japan's four chief islands.

life, he treated her to an exciting ride in his speedboat, on which he was the pilot.

Traveling far and wide had become a habit now. In 1955 she visited beautiful Bali, where it seemed to her she saw enough exotic dancing to last the rest of her life, and went on to the glamorous lands of Thailand and Cambodia. In 1957 she spent a month in the Soviet Union, climaxed in Yalta by a personal interview, through interpreters, with Premier Nikita Khrushchev.

"Can I tell our papers that we have had a friendly conversation?" Khrushchev demanded at the end of their recorded talk.

"You can say," she told him in her precise manner, "that we had a friendly conversation but that we differ."

"At least," he said, grinning, "we did not shoot each other."

There were other trips to distant lands, long and short. She visited Morocco in North Africa, another country newly independent. She attended the World's Fair in Brussels in 1958. She made a second trip to the Soviet Union, mainly to find out about treatment given to emotionally disturbed children. She went to Warsaw, Poland, for a meeting of the World Federation of United Nations Associations. Wherever she went she asked questions and insisted on seeing for herself, insofar as was possible, how the citizens lived, just as her husband had taught her to do many years before when she acted as his private investigator.

Her modesty and graciousness won her friends even among those who had decided in advance not to like her. As for the simple people, there was never any doubt of their feelings about her. They waited for hours to catch a glimpse of her, even in the rain. "Mees-ess Roose-velt! Mees-ess Roosevelt!" Their cries resounded around the world.

"She has walked with kings, but never lost the common touch," said an English reporter of this woman who was not young, nor stylish, nor beautiful, but who had the rare gift of being interested in others.

She loved every moment of her foreign travels, there is no doubt of that, but America was her home and that was where she always returned.

She listens respectfully to ninety-year-old Sir Shouson, one of Hong Kong's three Chinese Knights and financial leader of the Colony.

And in Yugoslavia she encourages President Tito to talk about problems and progress in his country.

IX. The Home Front

*"What we should seek, rather than gratitude
or love, is the respect of the world."*

It was Eleanor Roosevelt's private opinion that birthdays, her own at least, should go unnoticed. Her friends felt otherwise, and a thousand of them attended her seventieth birthday party, held at the Hotel Roosevelt in New York City, October, 1954. Among the guests were Trygve Lie, the first UN Secretary-General, Dag Hammarskjold, his successor, Ralph J. Bunche, UN Under-Secretary for Special Political Affairs; Bernard Baruch, and her old adversary, Soviet Foreign Minister Andrei Vishinsky. President Eisenhower wired his congratulations.

"No woman has ever so comforted the distressed, or so distressed the comfortable," said Clare Boothe Luce, American Ambassador to Rome, one of the cleverest remarks of the evening.

The best birthday present possible had been given to her five months earlier on May 17: the Supreme Court decision that racial segregation in schools was unconstitutional. There would be a long and thorny path between the decision and the realization of desegregation, but at least the barriers to that path were down.

At seventy, Mrs. Roosevelt's hair was almost white, and she was bothered by a slight deafness, but her energy was still boundless, at home as well as abroad. The interlacing of her foreign travels with American ones produced a startling pattern of contrasts. Nine days after the news-

reels showed Queen Juliana of the Netherlands rushing down the palace steps to embrace Mrs. Roosevelt, columnist Harry Golden watched her at a party of the inter-racial Highlander Folk School, in Monteagle, Tennessee. She was seated on a wooden bench, eating lunch from a paper plate, when a Negro mother asked her if she would mind being photographed with her child. Mrs. Roosevelt promptly put her lunch aside and held the little one on her lap until the picture-taking was over.

At her seventieth birthday party in the Hotel Roosevelt, New York City, she smiles at the guests as she prepares to cut her mammoth birthday cake.

In the peace and tranquillity of Val-Kill, near Hyde Park, Eleanor Roosevelt and Fala's grandson take an early morning stroll.

Her American speaking engagements averaged about one hundred each year. She spoke from coast to coast, from north to south, at luncheons, dinners, in halls and for open air meetings, and there was always a crowd. Sometimes she lectured in three widely separated cities — Baltimore, Chicago, and Detroit, for instance — in one day. Occasionally she sat up on a plane all night to keep an appointment. Once Franklin, Jr. discovered she had not been to bed the night before and scolded her.

"I have no aches and pains," she told him blithely. "And I'm perfectly happy."

Jet planes, which officially entered commercial aviation in 1959, served her better than any magic carpet.

Much of her interstate traveling was done for the American Association of the United Nations, which she had joined as a volunteer soon after her resignation as a UN delegate. The function of the AAUN was to build popular support for the United Nations. Mrs. Roosevelt's efforts were in part responsible for the organizing of more than two hundred local AAUN chapters.

For appointments in nearby towns, she traveled by train or bus. Around Hyde Park, though not in the city, she continued to drive her own car. During a blizzard, when she could not get it out of the garage, she hitchhiked from Hyde Park to Poughkeepsie, so as not to miss an engagement. There was one time when she agreed to speak to a very small group in a particularly inconvenient suburb.

"Why do you bother?" someone asked her.

"Because no one else will," she replied.

Within New York City she often used the subway. A young woman, seeing her hanging to a subway strap, jumped up excitedly to offer her seat. Mrs. Roosevelt took it for granted that the girl was merely being kind to an old lady.

When more convenient, she took taxis, which

Val-Kill was an ideal spot for picnics and the former First Lady held many of them. At this one, her guests are members of UNESCO, her friends at the United Nations.

resulted occasionally in surprising reunions. There was the driver who demanded: "Don't you remember me, Mrs. Roosevelt? I'm the guy who cooked lunch for you on Bora Bora."

Bora Bora was one of the remote island outposts in the Pacific which she had visited during the war some twenty years before.

Through radio and television, she magnified the audience she could reach with her pleas for a stronger UN, a more comprehensive civil rights program, more help for the underprivileged, a peaceful solution of the world's problems. She made some recordings, the best known being her narration of Prokofiev's *Peter and the Wolf,* which she did originally at Tanglewood, with the Boston Symphony Orchestra, and later in Japan.

As a speaker she had improved greatly since the time when Louis Howe gave his strident criticism. She had learned to lower her voice, and her diction was flawless. That she never became a polished orator was more than offset by her sincerity.

Her New York home was now an apartment in the East Seventies with two bedrooms, a kitchen,

Students in a ninth grade English class at PS 49, Brooklyn, listen attentively as Mrs. Roosevelt speaks to them about America's future.

and a living room. There was no dining room; guests, no matter how celebrated, ate from card tables or from trays, rather to the horror of her children. She was usually up at seven-thirty no matter how late she had retired, and at nine-thirty was at work.

One of her bedrooms was converted into an office. Here, with the aid of her secretary, she dictated *My Day,* her magazine articles, the books she wrote, alone or in collaboration with someone else, and answered an average of a hundred letters received daily.

Year after year, on January 31, Franklin D. Roosevelt's birthday, she participated in ceremonies for the March of Dimes campaign launched by her husband to fight polio. No cure for this crippling disease had been found, but in 1955 the first successful vaccine was licensed, named after Dr. Jonas Salk, who was responsible for it. That year Mrs. Roosevelt received $5000 with an award from the CIO Community Services Committee for "inspiring the American people to act in community affairs." She sent the money to the Warm Springs Foundation, requesting that half of it go to Dr. Salk for a vacation since "he looked tired."

The First International Conference on the "Peaceful Uses of Atomic Energy" was held in Geneva in 1955, and attended by nuclear scientists from many nations. In the years since Hiroshima, great progress had been made in development of radioactive isotopes, a by-product of atomic energy, which were proving of value in treating cancer and other diseases; in scientific and agricultural research, in improving industrial techniques. Thus the Conference opened the door for exchange of information between nations on ways in which atomic energy could benefit mankind — not destroy it.

In the summers, Mrs. Roosevelt spent much of her time at Val-Kill Cottage, where to an extent

In her New York apartment she entertains the Committee of Correspondence, whose women delegates come from countries all over the world.

her life was like that of any other suburban housewife. She wheeled a shopping cart through the local supermarket, walked her Scotty — the one who now replaced Fala — down a country road, picked up her mail at the Hyde Park post office, visited with her neighbors, and on Sunday mornings sat in the family pew at St. James Episcopal Church, where other Roosevelts before her had worshiped some one hundred and fifty years.

Her life differed from other women of the community because of the variety and the number of her visitors. Emperor Haile Selassie of Ethiopia and Prime Minister Nehru were just two of the world leaders who came to lay wreaths on the grave of Franklin D. Roosevelt in the Hyde Park rose garden, and stayed to enjoy the hospitality of Mrs. Roosevelt at Val-Kill.

Nikita Khrushchev paid her a visit both times he was in the United States. The first time he was rushed through so fast he barely had time to munch a bun, and all the food she had had prepared was divided among the army of police and troops who had escorted him. The second time he stayed to tea, and they had a long talk, once again not agreeing, yet not "shooting each other." A deluge of angry letters followed this visit, as though she had committed a crime in receiving the head of a great power whose system of government differed from her own.

Foreign notables were often surprised to find

With Premier and Mrs. Nikita Khrushchev, after the Soviet Premier has left a wreath on the grave of Franklin Roosevelt.

flowing with them, all no less lively than the young Roosevelts of a few decades past. It must have been compensation for her own lonely childhood to see them enjoying themselves.

She had never forgotten her childhood grief at the plight of New York's newsboys. In her speeches to groups in foreign lands, she frequently stressed the need for children to have time to play, to grow strong, to continue their education.

Mrs. Roosevelt was one of the sponsors of the Wiltwyck School for Boys, set up to combat this evil, an experimental inter-racial school for de-

A Christmas party for the boys of Faye Emerson Roosevelt (left),

her living so simply. In truth, the "cottage" with its twelve rooms and porches was more than sufficient for her needs. The wide grounds, encompassing a swimming pool, a tennis court, a wooded area, and a stream, were an ideal picnic site, utilized all summer long.

With equal graciousness, she entertained women's organizations, writers, unemployed actors, personal friends, friends of friends, busloads of school children, and large groups of college students. Exchange students from foreign lands were always welcome. She once held a picnic for seventy-five United Nations employees. Food was simple, but there were always more eggs to scramble when unexpected guests arrived.

She had never tried to interfere with the lives of her children, but she held open house for her nineteen grandchildren and (by 1957) nine great-grandchildren. The cottage was frequently over-

linquent, neglected, or mentally troubled youths. She raised money for them, brought them Harry Belafonte and other performers, and once each summer invited some one hundred and fifty Wiltwyck boys to the cottage for a picnic.

These offspring of city slums and broken homes were her children too. She played games with them, read them Kipling's "How the Elephant Got His Trunk," and served them hot dogs, soft drinks, and ice cream. When told that she should not bother to butter their rolls, she shrugged.

"I did so for the King and Queen of England. Should I do less for these boys?"

Wiltwyck School. Her daughter-in-law, helps to distribute presents.

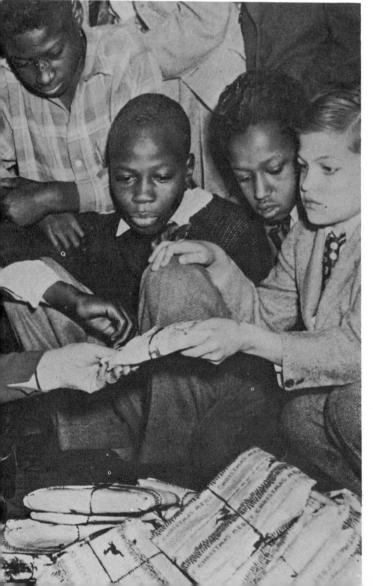

Mrs. Roosevelt and John F. Kennedy, the youngest elected President in American history, elected in the closest presidential race in history.

Her interest in politics continued. She supported Adlai Stevenson for President in 1952 and 1956 and tried, in 1960, to persuade the Democratic National Convention to nominate him for a third time. When Senator John F. Kennedy was nominated instead, her first reaction was keen disappointment.

On August 14, 1960, the twenty-fifth anniversary of the Social Security Act, Senator Kennedy visited her at Val-Kill. She talked to him at length, finding him, perhaps to her surprise, a brilliant man, hospitable to new ideas and, she judged with an upsurge of hope, truly desirous of helping his countrymen and helping humanity as well. She made up her mind. Though she was seventy-six and not too well any more, she campaigned for him actively. At his inauguration, January 20, 1961, she was offered an honor seat on the presidential stand. Smilingly, she refused, watching the ceremony instead in the lower section reserved for the diplomatic corps.

"I can hear better here," she explained.

[85]

X. First Lady of the World

*"You have to do the best you can in this world
and when you have done that, that is all you can do."*

Soon after assuming office, President Kennedy nominated Mrs. Roosevelt as one of the five United States delegates to the United Nations Fifteenth Assembly, with which Adlai Stevenson served as chief of the U.S. Mission. Visitors to "UN-Ville" hovered around, hoping for a glimpse of this tall, white-haired woman with the friendly smile. It seemed right that she should be there again.

The twentieth century had seen many women rise to prominence in fields where once they had been forbidden or discouraged.

Women writers — Willa Cather, Dorothy Canfield Fisher, Pearl Buck, Edna Ferber, Dorothy Parker, Katherine Anne Porter, among many others — had achieved success with no need to hide beneath a man's name as the Brontë sisters and George Eliot had done. Margaret Mead, an anthropologist, and Rachel Carson, a biologist, had proved themselves both as writers and scientists.

There were women artists with talents as diversified as that of Georgia O'Keefe, with her stark desert scenes, and of Grandma Moses, the little old lady whose primitives of farm life had enchanted the art world. Margaret Bourke-White had taken top honors in photography. Helen Keller had shown that intelligence can transcend the dark silent world of the deaf and blind. Jacqueline Cochrane, an aviator like Amelia Earhart, became the first woman to fly faster than sound.

The theatre had produced Helen Hayes, Ethel Barrymore, Katharine Cornell, while the motion picture stars who had achieved fame and fortune were legion. A twenty-year-old Negro girl, Wilma Rudolph, had triumphed in three races of the 1960 Olympics at Rome.

Helen Keller — one of many twentieth century women of achievement.

She was seventy-six when she addressed a Los Angeles audience during the 1960 presidential campaign. She was sure it would be the last time she would participate. "After all, next time I will be eighty and that would be absurd."

[87]

Women were earning their living as physicians, surgeons, psychiatrists, dentists, architects, lawyers, engineers, business executives, and in practically every branch of science. Ninety-eight per cent of America's 460,000 nurses were women, an approximate 98 per cent increase from 1900. More than 500,000 women were working for the federal government, making up a fourth of the labor force of America's largest single employer. A smattering of this half million women were in high-level posts.

To Eleanor Roosevelt, this was not enough. At the outset of his tenure, she sent President Kennedy a three-page list of women whom she believed qualified for really important government positions. There was no immediate response.

One of the President's first concerns was to give new impetus to the foreign aid program, which, it was widely believed, would in the long run bring new markets for United States goods. Proposed by the President and authorized by Congress was Aid for International Development (with the appropriate initials AID), created to unify and expand existing foreign aid agencies. AID meant a new school for Bolivian children on the shore of 12,000-foot high Lake Titicaca. It meant the reforestation of a barren mountain in Tunisia. It meant loans for housing, for locomotives, for industrial machinery. AID, working with the UN specialized agencies, meant more teachers, doctors, and nurses, more "Food for Peace" for those to whom hunger had always been a way of life.

Not even the AID captured the popular imagination as did the President's Peace Corps, set up under the Department of State in March, 1961. Peace Corps members were a new kind of army, who would go to far countries not to wage wars but to make friends. They would eat the same food, live the same way, and speak the same language as the native citizens, and work with them and for them side by side. Within a few hours after the Peace Corps was announced, its headquarters had more volunteers than could be handled. Surprisingly, it seemed that America was full of idealists, to whom money was less important than doing something worth while.

Eleanor Roosevelt was on the Advisory Council of the Peace Corps, and she invited the President to discuss it on her educational TV program, "Prospects of Mankind." This was the sort of thing about which she could be truly enthusiastic. In her own fashion she had been a Peace Corps worker for years.

The "cold war" still loomed as a threat to the very survival of humanity. In 1959, she had been one of twenty-two prominent Americans to send a joint letter to Eisenhower, Macmillan, England's Prime Minister, and Khrushchev, urging an immediate agreement on a treaty banning nuclear tests. As founder and honorary chairman of the Americans for Democratic Action, she urged United States recognition and a UN seat for Communist China. China, with its 669 million people, was by far the largest country in the world. Was it not folly, she reasoned, to think one could ignore it forever? Almost exclusively now, her *My Day* was devoted to political and world affairs. She was still accused of mixing too much in "controversial" matters. But then, unemployment insurance, old age pensions, and many other of her early causes had once been considered controversial but had now won general acceptance.

The list of charitable organizations she supported in one way or another was endless. To only one did she give her name, the Eleanor Roosevelt Cancer Foundation, which was dedicated to building new cancer research facilities and setting up an international fellowship research program.

In May, she was named honorary chairman of the "Tractors for Freedom Committee," organized

Peace Corps worker Richard Lipez, of Lock Haven, Pennsylvania, gives his Ethiopian students lessons in English. In return they teach him their dialect and their customs.

to raise money for the release of the prisoners held in Cuba after the ill-fated Bay of Pigs invasion. The project collapsed when Cuba's Fidel Castro raised his demands prohibitively. All donations had to be returned and the enormous amount of work went for nothing. The prisoners spent more months in captivity before a new release plan could be worked out.

By September she was busy with politics again, working with Senator Herbert H. Lehman, a very old friend, against Tammany Hall politicians, just as her husband had done when he was New York State Senator. In November, she accepted a presidential appointment on the "Freedom from Hunger Foundation," to work with the UN. Mrs. Woodrow Wilson and former President Truman served with her.

President Kennedy had not forgotten her appeal for more women in government posts. In December, he announced a new Commission on the Status of Women, to study ways to eliminate "all barriers to the full partnership of women in our democracy." Mrs. Roosevelt was made chairman. She considered this her last major activity, but the "minor" activities did not lessen. That month the Gallup Poll reported that she was the woman "most admired by Americans" in 1961. It was the thirteenth time in fourteen years she had been so designated.

Over the years she had received a succession of awards, but none pleased her more than the Nansen Medal, which she received for her outstanding work "in behalf of refugees." The medal was named after the Norwegian Arctic explorer, Fridjof Nansen, who had himself saved the lives of many refugees in his work with the League of Nations after the First World War.

Although she had had no formal education, she was made an honorary member of Phi Beta Kappa, and in all received thirty-four honorary degrees from universities at home and abroad,

Back in the UN harness. Mrs. Roosevelt sits next to Ambassador Adlai E. Stevenson, head of the U. S. delegation, at the 15th regular session of the UN General Assembly, March 7, 1961.

among them Smith College in America, Oxford University in England, and the University of Utrecht in the Netherlands.

The "Space Age," launched officially when the Soviet Union put Sputnik I into orbit in 1957, was now well under way. There was wild excitement when John Glenn became the first American to orbit the earth, on February 20, 1962. Scott Carpenter's similar feat on May 24 was greeted with no less a combination of advance fears, awe, and rejoicing. A purely American triumph was the communications satellite, *Telstar,* launched on July 10, which recorded the first transatlantic television broadcasts. Space probes and incredibly sensitive instruments were bringing back more facts about the moon, Mars, and Venus. In this second half of the twentieth century, the universe was revealing some of its long-kept secrets.

In July, 1962, Mrs. Roosevelt held her last picnic for the boys of the Wiltwyck School. Before they left, she passed out gifts of candy. As the boys crowded around her, her hair was in her eyes, her tennis shoes were streaked with grass stains, but her face was radiant.

By August 26, the forty-second anniversary of the adoption of the nineteenth amendment on woman suffrage, she sent the President a progress report on the Commission on the Status of Women. On its agenda was an endorsement of the principle of equal pay for men and women on the same jobs. Already twenty-two states had equal pay laws, but she would not live to see the federal equal pay law.

A new book, *Eleanor Roosevelt's Book of Common Sense Etiquette,* was on press. Another one, significantly called *"Tomorrow Is Now,"* was nearly finished. She interceded with the immigration authorities for a couple who had adopted an orphan in Athens, Greece, and were having trouble getting permission to bring the child home

[91]

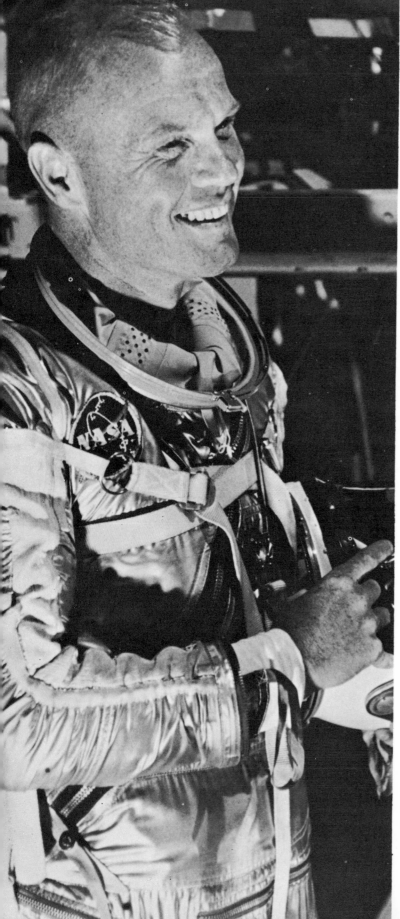

with them. With the NAACP she was trying to save the life of a fifteen-year-old Georgia youth, Preston Cobb, Jr., condemned to death for murder. (There would later be an appeal.)

Toward the end of August, she agreed to tour Queens for several Democratic reform candidates in the September 6 primary.

"I must have picked up a bug of some kind," she told the young law student who called for her. "You'll have to steady me when I get out of the car." Her temperature was almost 102.

At their first stop, a group of children presented her with a bouquet of flowers. "You see," she told her escort, beaming, "I had to come. They expected me."

At a rally later in the evening several boys darted up to the speaker's stand on which she had climbed with difficulty. "How's your old friend Khrushchev, Eleanor?" one of them yelled jeeringly.

Some of the reform Democrats wanted to go after the hecklers, but their guest of honor shook her head. "They are either being paid for their rudeness, or they do not know what they are doing," she said.

This was her last public appearance.

On September 26, the newspapers mentioned that Mrs. Roosevelt had entered the Columbia Presbyterian Medical Center for a routine checkup. She had so long been a tower of strength, no one could believe it was serious. Later, when it was announced that she was suffering from anemia and a lung infection, letters began to pour in, not only from her friends but from countless persons who had never met her.

One week after her seventy-eighth birthday, on October 18, she was released from the hospital.

Project Mercury Astronaut John H. Glenn, Jr., wearing his pressure suit. "I don't know what you can say about a day when you see four beautiful sunsets," he commented of his orbital flight.

She knew she was not cured, but she wanted to return to the familiar surroundings of her New York apartment. Adlai Stevenson was the only friend outside her family who was admitted to see her. The end came at 6:15 P.M., on November 7, 1962.

United States flags everywhere flew at half-mast, the first time this honor had been accorded to the widow of a President. Three American Presidents — Eisenhower, Truman, and Kennedy — attended the ceremony when she was laid to rest in the Hyde Park rose garden, next to her husband. Representatives of the one hundred and ten countries of the United Nations came too, speaking foreign tongues, and some wearing the native dress of the new African nations. Glowing and eloquent tributes poured in from great personages the world over.

None would have appealed to her more than the comment of a truck driver from the Bronx.

"The folks will miss her," he said. "She was always on their side."

A group of school children from P.S. 233, in Brooklyn, sent Ambassador Adlai Stevenson a "Remembrance Book" about her. "Eleanor Roosevelt was like a mother to the world and we are like orphans because of her death," wrote one of these youthful students.

The poor, the oppressed, the sick, the physically handicapped, the unhappy — those were the ones to whom her loss would be greatest. For over half a century they had turned to her with their troubles, knowing she would always listen, always seek a way to help them. It would not be easy to do without her.

Eleanor Roosevelt was like a mother to the world and we are like orphans because of her death

WROTE A YOUTHFUL STUDENT
PUBLIC SCHOOL 233 NEW YORK

The flag of the United Nations flies at half-mast.

[93

*The Declaration of Human Rights was in large part
the result of the patience, perseverance, and wisdom of Eleanor Roosevelt.
As a social document, it ranks in importance with the English Magna Carta
and the American Bill of Rights.*